Endorsements for

Leora's Dexter Stories: The Scarcity Years of the Great Depression

Many of us have had relatives that saved every little thing to the point of ridicule. When you laughingly tell people about it, the response is, "They lived in the depression, didn't they?" And yes, it's true. When I'd open a certain cupboard in my Gramma's kitchen, there would be an avalanche of Cool Whip containers or Parkay butter tubs. Funny to us, but not to them. In this book, Joy shows us what it was really like, and in an Iowa area where I lived myself for some time. Thanks, Joy, for the reality check!

—**Van Harden,** author, speaker, and
Marconi Award-winning broadcaster

My maternal grandparents, immigrants from the Netherlands and Germany, raised twelve children through the Great Depression. Much of who I am today was shaped by lessons my mother learned during those difficult years. Reading *Leora's Dexter Stories* provided a heart-warming emotional reunion with my mother and grandmother as I recalled their related stories of dealing with disappointments, heartache and even joy in the face of adversity.

From early in the book I was held captive by this loving and tenacious woman named Leora. The author has woven her grandmother›s story into a written tapestry that reveals Leora and her family for the reader to know and appreciate. Joy Neal Kidney›s grandmother and her letters are a testimony to the strength, devotion and creativity of Iowa›s rural women.

—**Arvid Huisman,** former newspaper publisher,
author of *More Country Roads*, an anthology selected
from more than 900 of his Country Road columns,
which continue today in *Iowa History Journal*

Leora (Goff) Wilson was a prolific letter writer. The Iowa farm wife whose life spanned nearly a full century was also a resourceful and devoted wife and mother whose resilience carried her through the heartbreak of losing children—both as infants and as young adults—through disease and war. She left behind a trove of memoir-worthy information that provided the basis for *Leora's Letters*, set during World War II.

Author Kidney once again dives into family letters and tales to give us an unblinking look at the two decades that preceded the Second World War. Kidney's deft touch shows how Leora's unflagging pragmatism and love of family were steadying anchors in her family's constant struggle with unemployment, illness, severe weather, government assistance, and the general harshness of life in the Great Depression years.

To many readers, *Leora's Dexter Stories* may seem like tales from a distant past. To others, they may conjure up much more recent memories. All should be grateful to Leora for documenting her experiences and to Kidney for sharing them.

—**Larry Lehmer,** journalist and author of *The Day the Music Died: The Last Tour of Buddy Holly, the Big Bopper, and Ritchie Valens*

Joy never forgets that the biggest part of history is "story." She has a gift for transforming the facts of one Iowa farm family's struggles, joys and tremendous sacrifices during the Great Depression and World War 2 into significant stories of grit, resourcefulness and power of the human spirit. We live in a world shaped by the World War II generation's courage, personal responsibility, humility, work ethic, commitment, integrity and service to others.

If you wish to make a positive impact with your own life, there's no better place to find inspiration than in the lives of the Wilson family.

—**Darcy Dougherty Maulsby,** Iowa's Storyteller, author of several books, including *A Culinary History of Iowa*, and *Dallas County* (which includes the Wilsons's WWII story)

For the duration of her book, *Leora's Dexter Stories: The Scarcity Years of the Great Depression*, Joy Neal Kidney allows us to become members—or at least neighbors—of the Wilson family: Leora, Clabe, and their seven children. We couldn't be in better company. The Wilson family deal heroically with hardships, including the death of their young twins from whooping cough, the shortage of food, and a landlady "mean enough to drown kittens." Kidney's prose is clean, honest, and sometimes poetic. Handsome photographs add to the intimacy of this heart-lifting book.

—**Betty Moffett** taught for nearly 30 years in Grinnell College›s Writing Lab, and is the author of *Coming Clean*, a collection of short stories, published by Ice Cube Press

Joy has captured a slice of Iowa history through the engaging story of her family during the Great Depression. The era is brought to life by her ability to weave primary sources and firsthand accounts throughout the narrative. A great read!

—**Cheryl Mullenbach,** author of *The Great Depression for Kids* among other books, and regular contributor to *Iowa History Journal*

I grew up in Dallas County hearing the stressing and often poignant stories of the struggle, disappointment, and survival lived and witnessed by my own family in the Depression, some of whom are mentioned in Joy's book. These stories helped shape me and send me on a life-long path of searching for the past and the lessons learned from it. Leora's Dexter Stories is not only an excellent read, but a valuable historic resource of this incredibly important time in our history.

—**Mark A. Peitzman,** historian and preservationist, formerly with the State Historical Society of Iowa and the Iowa Department of Cultural Affairs

Leora's Dexter Stories is an eye-opening Depression Era history of one small-town family in tough times. The Wilson kids grew up in the very dot on a map where I grew up during the 1960s. Joy's book has caused me to look at my hometown with even more appreciation of its past.

—**Rod Stanley,** Oral historian, Dexter Museum Board

Insightful glimpse into the daily lives of Iowa's rural poor during the early twentieth century . . . Skillfully addresses the often-overlooked experiences of childhood . . . Joy Neal Kidney's descriptive storytelling causes the reader to feel the Wilson family's tragedies and triumphs.

—**Matthew R. Walsh,** author of *The Good Governor: Robert Ray and the Indochinese Refugees of Iowa*

Leora's Dexter Stories

THE SCARCITY YEARS OF THE GREAT DEPRESSION

JOY NEAL KIDNEY

LEGACY
p r e s s

Published by Legacy Press
Your life tells a story; we can help you write it.
www.legacypress.org

Printed in the United States of America

Library of Congress Control Number:

ISBN (softcover): 978-1-7341587-2-4
ISBN (ebook): 978-1-7341587-3-1
ISBN (hardcover): 978-1-7341587-6-2

Available from Amazon.com and other retail outlets

Cover design and interior design and layout by Nelly Murariu at PixBeeDesign.com
Author photo by Emina Hastings
Dexter map and family chart by Cari Wooten-Fuller and Nelly Murariu

For Kate

He raises the poor from the dust,
And lifts the needy from the ash heap.

PSALM 113:7

Table of Contents

Foreword
John Busbee

The sharing of personal histories introduces us to new people, places and times. *Leora's Dexter Stories: The Scarcity Years* delivers a compelling narrative that stirs the embers slumbering within our memory's hearth, enflaming a special connection between two histories—the author's and ours. This magical blending of two worlds creates a journey both familiar and fresh for the reader. Joy Neal Kidney gives us an exceptional hybrid story of her family's history as it unfolded during a challenging time in American history.

Leora Wilson's family is tested during our country's most challenging times in the 20th century: The Great Depression. Through their tenacity and caring for each other, Leora's life is steeped in a survivalism grit, as so many other American families also endured. Kidney anchors her grandmother's stories through oral and written remembrances of her own mother, Leora's daughter, Doris, and her uncle, Delbert. Each chapter in *Leora's Dexter Stories: The Scarcity Years,* adds to a rich, personal understanding of a time when more than a third of America suffered under harsh conditions, both economically and environmentally. Through these trials and tribulations shines this family's unquenchable hopes and dreams, conveyed with gratitude, grace and perseverance. Just as Leora used scraps of cloth to patch bib overalls, bed clothes and dresses, Kidney lovingly stitches together a revealing historical patchwork of images, oral history, letters, news stories and more into an immensely satisfying immersion into a time that continues to resonate today.

With enough glimpses into the reality of these difficult times, Kidney provides a ground zero impact of how such economic challenges affected her Iowa ancestors. We get to know the Wilson family, its relatives of that era, friends and community members.

Losses and struggles are intertwined with love and aspirations, in no small part by Leora Wilson's determined vision for her definitions of success: her children graduating from high school and a warm, loving home wherever their family totem, the velvet "Home Sweet Home" picture, hangs. To share this journey with the Wilsons is to better understand The Great Depression, an Iowa family surviving those tempestuous times, and perhaps better understand our own family history.

Snuggle into a favorite chair with a warm cup of tea and drift into Leora's stories as Joy lovingly channels those remembrances into a fulfilling book. Kidney feeds the flames of family, home and setting. We receive its comfort. To experience history on such a personal level feeds our souls, and we find ourselves better prepared for the now and future.

> — **John Busbee,** The Culture Buzz, Iowa Governor's Award for Partnership & Collaboration in the Arts, Iowa History Award for "Last Measure of Full Devotion," *Iowa History Journal*

Preface

The Clabe and Leora Wilson family of Dallas County, Iowa, had seven children when the Great Depression deepened. They were a farm family who'd already lost land after the Great War. By the time of the Stock Market Crash of 1929, they were already feeling the pinch.

Clabe said that it took so little for Leora's happiness—healthy, thriving children who were doing well in school. She was an uncomplicated woman with straightforward goals: a home of their own, surrounded by family, and high school diplomas for her children. She was determined to do the hard work to accomplish her mission.

This is a look at an important era in world, national, and local history—the undertow of the Great Depression—through the lens of one family.

Between 1926 and 1939, the Wilson family moved at least eight times. Daughter Doris, when trying to recall decades later, couldn't remember for sure whether they lived in one of the shabby houses two or three times.

This is a true story, inspired by my grandmother's hand-written memoirs and old letters, plus stories from other family members. I've used narrative techniques of scene and dialogue based on their own stories, to help picture what life was like for one small-town family during these bleak years of history.

1930 DEXTER MAP

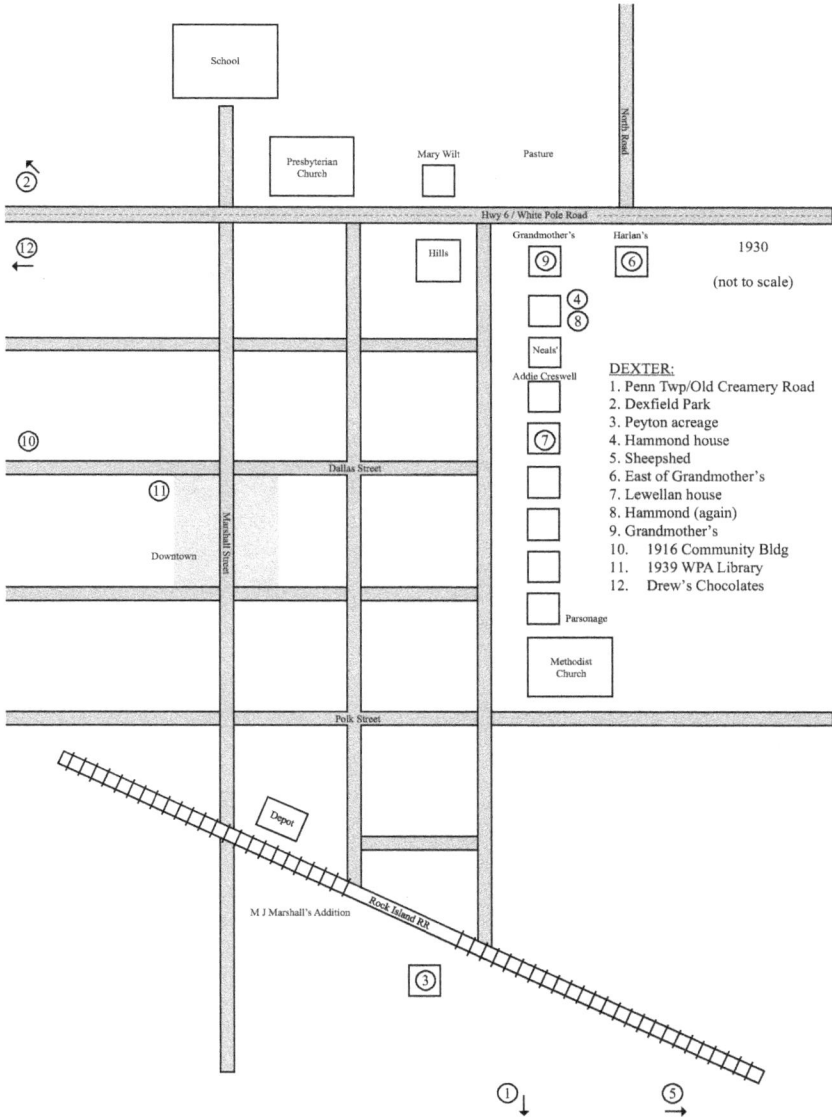

School

Presbyterian
Church

Mary Wilt

Pasture

North Road

Hwy 6 / White Pole Road

②

⑫

Hills

Grandmother's

⑨

Harlan's

⑥

1930

(not to scale)

④
⑧

Neals'

Addie Creswell

⑩

⑦

Dallas Street

⑪

Marshall Street

Downtown

Parsonage

Methodist
Church

DEXTER:
1. Penn Twp/Old Creamery Road
2. Dexfield Park
3. Peyton acreage
4. Hammond house
5. Sheepshed
6. East of Grandmother's
7. Lewellan house
8. Hammond (again)
9. Grandmother's
10.   1916 Community Bldg
11.   1939 WPA Library
12.   Drew's Chocolates

Polk Street

Depot

M J Marshall's Addition

Rock Island RR

③

①

⑤

GOFF FAMILY CHART

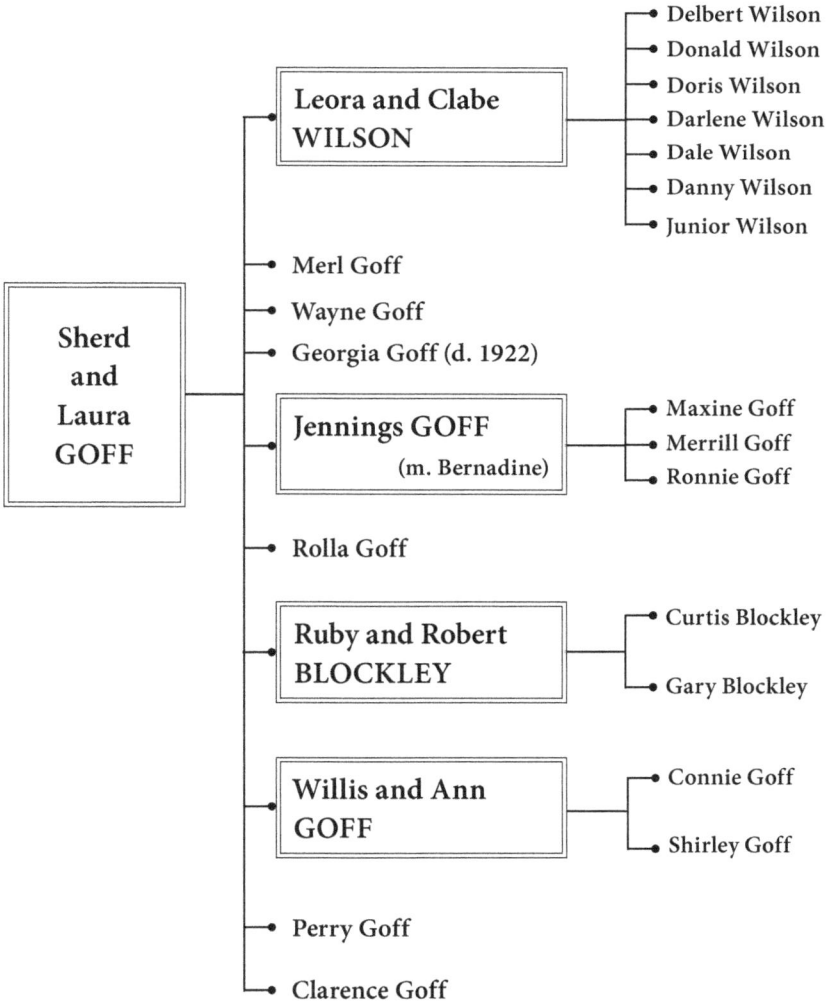

Sherd and Laura GOFF

- **Leora and Clabe WILSON**
  - Delbert Wilson
  - Donald Wilson
  - Doris Wilson
  - Darlene Wilson
  - Dale Wilson
  - Danny Wilson
  - Junior Wilson
- Merl Goff
- Wayne Goff
- Georgia Goff (d. 1922)
- **Jennings GOFF** (m. Bernadine)
  - Maxine Goff
  - Merrill Goff
  - Ronnie Goff
- Rolla Goff
- **Ruby and Robert BLOCKLEY**
  - Curtis Blockley
  - Gary Blockley
- **Willis and Ann GOFF**
  - Connie Goff
  - Shirley Goff
- Perry Goff
- Clarence Goff

CHAPTER 1

◆

Danny's Earache

The country school's bell fell silent for the summer of 1927. Orange lilies had emerged along the rural road bank in Penn Township, along with wild blue violets. The five older Wilson children were students there. Danny visited school one day that spring, getting him in the mind of starting first grade in the fall.

The farm economy. That was the problem. During the last war, farmers were urged to borrow money to buy more land, in hopes of big profits.

That wrong speculation caused farmers to suffer.

Clabe and Leora Wilson lost almost everything, and he was glad to find work as a tenant farmer near Dexter, Iowa.

Home was Leora's favorite place, among her family, with everyone healthy.

In her cotton house dress and apron, Leora fried a dinner of sausage patties for Clabe and their seven children, ages two to twelve. Hot lard sizzled in a heavy cast iron skillet on the black kitchen range. A pot of green beans with onions simmered on the huge stove, about ready to serve along with a big salad of leaf lettuce from their lush garden. Doris, age eight, who had helped snap those green beans, set the table with a plate in front of each chair. Her younger sister Darlene minded Danny and toddler Junior.

Danny whined. Maybe he'd missed his mamma while she was gone. Leora and little Junior had just gotten back from Kansas City, where she'd been with her folks and her brother, Jennings Goff, to see their younger brother and meet his new wife—Willis and Ann.

1

Their sister Ruby took care of four of Leora's youngsters, while the older boys, Delbert and Donald stayed on the farm with their dad.

Junior, Danny, twins Darlene and Dale, Doris, Donald, and Delbert Wilson. 1927, Penn Township, Madison County, Iowa

Sherd and Laura Goff, Leora Wilson with Junior. Kansas City, Spring 1927

Clabe and the two older boys, all wearing bib overalls, washed up in the enamel pan on the porch. Their dog Husky stayed outside. The screen door cried out as the boys and their dad sauntered in, hanging caps on pegs and wiping their shoes on the rag rug.

"Yum, sausage!" Delbert swept up little Danny, who'd continued to whimper against his mother's skirt. "I remember when we butchered last winter and helped make this sausage, cranking the handle to that grinder."

Sausage was made with three parts of lean meat, one part fat, plus seasonings, then put through a grinder.

"And rendered the lard." Leora scooped up the savory patties onto a plate. "Remember when Danny stuck his arm into one of those big five-gallon crocks of it and stirred it?" Everyone laughed.

Clabe boosted Junior into his highchair and cut up some green beans and sausage for him. Twelve-year-old Delbert kept Danny on his lap as he ate. Danny wasn't very hungry.

After the meal, Clabe raked back his chair, reached for his pipe and Prince Albert. He tamped a little tobacco into the bowl of pipe. He struck a wooden match on the bottom of his shoe. It popped into flame, which he held into the pipe. Clabe inhaled through the stem several times until it caught.

"Danny, come here." Pipe in hand, Clabe reached for the mewling boy. Danny held up his arms for a lift onto his father's lap. "What's the problem, little feller? Did you miss your momma?"

Danny leaned against his dad, quietly pulling on an ear.

"Leora, do you think he might have an earache?"

"Might be. Why don't you try warm smoke and see if it helps."

Clabe had Danny sit up so he could blow warm smoke in his ear. All the eyes at the table watched. Danny settled back against the bib of his dad's overalls, seemingly better.

After dinner, the older boys left for the barn with their dad, while Doris and Darlene helped their mother scrape dishes as water heated to wash them. The three younger boys played with Husky right outside.

"Yoo-hoo, Mrs. Wilson!" Mrs. Wolfe appeared at the door. She'd walked up the dusty road. "Are you done with dinner? Is this a good time for a little visit?"

"You bet. I just put the dishes in the sink to soak. Let's rest our bones on the porch where it's cooler." Flanked by Leora's stickery ferns and Moses-in-the-Cradle plants, the chairs groaned like weary floorboards as the friends rocked.

"I want to hear all about your trip to Kansas City."

Danny shuffled around the corner of the house to find his mother.

"Oh, we just love Willis's new wife." Leora gathered the unhappy boy into her lap. "Her folks are just as nice as they can be, and live in a dandy house." Danny held his ear while she rocked.

"Does your son have an earache?" asked Mrs. Wolfe.

"Maybe so. Clabe blew warm smoke in it after dinner. It seemed to soothe but I guess it didn't last."

"Let me see," the neighbor offered. "Oh, Mrs. Wilson, there's a bulge. I think your boy may have a mastoid infection."

"Land sakes! There *is* a bulge. Doris!" she called. Doris appeared at the screen door. "Go find your dad in the barn. We need to take Danny to the doctor."

Clabe quickly changed out of his overalls and cranked up the Model T. He and little Danny made haste up the gravel road to town.

CHAPTER 2

Mastoidectomy

The doctor confirmed Mrs. Wolfe's diagnosis. Mastoiditis.

Clabe left his automobile with his in-laws in town, asking them to telephone Leora. Most homes in town and in rural areas had telephones by then, but not all had been wired for electricity. Laura Goff rang up her daughter to let her know that Clabe and Danny would leave on the next train for Methodist Hospital in Des Moines.

Families were usually on party lines, along with several others. If they wanted to make a call, they took down the receiver from a crank telephone, which was mounted on a wall. If someone was already on the line, the new caller had to wait.

Leora's folks, Sherd and Laura Goff, lived in the town of Dexter, three miles north. Leora's younger sister, two brothers, and the two children of one of the brothers, a widower, also lived with the Goffs. They'd also lost land during the slump in farm prices after the war.

What a comfort to live near extended family, but what a long day on the farm for Leora to wait for news. Delbert broke down in tears.

Clabe finally came home alone. He described how the doctor cut away the bone in order to drain the mastoid. He'd gotten to watch the operation! What a relief to find out that Danny would be all right. The nurses said it would be best not to visit, that he'd get upset and cry to go home. They assured Clabe that they'd take good care of him.

So, as hard as it was, for ten days their four-year-old stayed in the hospital thirty-five miles away. Leora telephoned every day to see how he fared. Fine, just fine, the nurses told her.

The day Danny was allowed to come home, the smaller children stayed with Grandmother in town, Clabe. Leora, and the three oldest youngsters, all dressed up and wearing hats, drove to Des Moines to get him. Danny, his head all bandaged, spotted them when they walked into the room. He stood up in the bed with his arms out, crayons spilling everywhere. He began to laugh and cry at the same time. Tears ran down his little face as he climbed down and scurried into his mother's embrace. "Momma, I saw your hat!"

Leora snapped a photo of the family just outside Methodist Hospital, Clabe holding Danny. Donald was already in the car. On their way home, which took about an hour, Danny sat on his mother's lap. He kept showing her his hands. "A nurse painted my nails."

Doris, Clabe holding Danny, Delbert, Donald is in the back seat of the Model T. Methodist Hospital, Des Moines, Iowa, 1927

Every day Clabe cranked up the automobile to take Danny to the Dexter doctor to have the bandages changed. After ten days, they returned to Des Moines for a checkup.

It was good to have Danny well again, and things back to normal. Well, the kids were healthy, but their relationship with the landlords faltered. The Wilsons had lived at this place south of Dexter not six months, but they had already commenced to wonder whether it had been a mistake. For some reason, the landlords seemed to resent them.

CHAPTER 3

Penn Township

Confrontation caused Clabe discomfort. The former landlord, where Clabe farmed for three years, had made suggestions that made Clabe uneasy. Along the Rock Island railroad tracks, which defined the north edge of that last farm, sat a pile of railroad ties.

"The railroad wouldn't miss a few," the landlord had suggested.

"Leora, I don't like that," he told his wife later. "It's just not right."

"Then tell him," she answered. "If he wants to do it, he can go get them himself."

Late that fall, another farmer complimented Clabe on his straight rows, and how neat he'd kept the farmyard. He asked what Clabe was being paid, and offered him more.

So at the end of harvesting in 1927, the Wilsons moved to a house in Penn Township. But they found a filthy house was filthy, even with bedbugs. Leora and Clabe scrubbed the whole place. When the bedsteads and springs arrived, Grandmother advised placing a can of kerosene under each bed leg to keep the bugs from climbing up into their mattresses. Grandmother knew plenty of handy tricks from moving from house to house through the decades.

For four Wilson beds, that meant sixteen cans of the smelly liquid, which was also used in the lamps in the house, and in lanterns outdoors. The house had no electricity. The acrid kerosene odor permeated the house when they finally got moved in after dark.

The scrubbing and the move exhausted Leora. She also had endured a miscarriage and was miserable enough to go to the doctor, who put her in the hospital overnight.

Was the extra pay for Clabe's farming skills worth all this trouble right before Christmas?

The kids dressed for school beside the warm stove, pulling on overalls and dresses over long underwear and winter stockings. Husky followed the five oldest as they hiked the country road to the rural school on the corner not half a mile south. Delbert and Donald were sixth-graders at the Penn Township school. Doris was the only one in third grade, so she studied with the fourth-graders. Twins Dale and Darlene joined the first graders.

Delbert soon got into a fight with Howard Davidson, the biggest kid in the school. Delbert won. The boys became fast friends.

Penn No. 4 School, four miles south of Dexter, 1927. Front: Harold Jobst, Charles Davidson, Fred Morford Jr., a Linn child, Darlene and Dale Wilson (1st graders), Marjery Wolf, a Linn child. Middle: Donald Wilson (6th grade), Lee Barr, Paul Willrich, Robert Davidson, Ivan Barr (peeking around Darlene), a Linn child, Doris Wilson (only one in 3rd grade), a Linn child. Back: Delbert Wilson (6th grade), a Linn child Linn, teacher Hazel Wetrich, Howard Davidson, Ray Thrailkill, Ilene Jensen, a Linn child.

The Wilson kids felt settled into the new shelter when their dad hung the velvet Home Sweet Home picture with roses their mother had painted before they were married, along with their oval wedding portraits, the 1910 composite picture of her sewing class, and a plate rail to display pretty things. Leora's abundance of green and viney houseplants always made any place they lived seem like home.

Mrs. Connrardy's Sewing School, 1910. Leora is to the right of the house.

The six-weeks sewing school came in handy. Leora had bought the treadle sewing machine when they lived at the last farm. Working the treadle like a teeter totter, she sewed clothes for her two daughters. That winter the machine whirred, as she made Christmas dresses with gold braid around the cuffs and collars—red for Darlene, Christmas green for Doris.

Every Christmas eve each Wilson child fastened a stocking to his own chair at the table, anticipating a treasure from Santa. That Christmas Doris received a two-headed doll with one body in her stocking. The heads screwed on—a baby one (Mary Etta, with a hood) and a girl one (Donna Zetta, which had a bonnet). Darlene's stocking also held a doll, one with what she called a "momma thing" in it, that cried when she leaned the doll forward.

Donald discovered a hatchet with a retractable cover in his stocking. Delbert found a harmonica. The big boys also got skis with which they made tracks to the barn, watering them down to make them slicker and faster to get to their chores.

The family settled in for a frosty Iowa winter, with leaden skies, drab and dreary. It turned into a tense season with the farm owner. He'd been affable with Clabe at first, maybe seemed too nice, but before long he began to borrow Clabe's tools, then forget to return them.

And the landlady had phoned Leora to let her know she didn't want the kids climbing in the trees. What would she complain about next?

◆

CHAPTER 4

Independence Day at Dexfield Park

Danny was doing well by Independence Day. "Get your lipstick on, Leorie," Clabe said. "Let's step out a little and take in the holiday at Dexfield Park."

Delbert and Donald spent their earnings on a few firecrackers from a local general store. They set them off in the yard while wearing their best knickers, waiting for the rest of the family to get ready to drive to the park. They'd both made money by helping in the field, riding the cultivator behind a team of horses, picking cherries for a neighbor, and also other odd jobs.

Leora's father loved going to any circus or fair, so they stopped in town to pick him up. Since Junior was too young to go along, he stayed with Grandmother while the rest drove to the park north of town.

"Grandpa, what do you think about Lindbergh?" Delbert had been keen on Charles Lindbergh ever since the pilot's historic solo flight across the Atlantic that spring.

"He's a brave man, isn't he?" said Sherd.

"Sure is. Boy, I'd like to be a flyer like that someday."

"I always wanted to be in the circus," said his grandfather. "That's why I like to go to Dexfield Park with you. There will be acrobatics and everything."

Built along the Raccoon River in 1915, the year of Delbert's birth, Dexfield was an early amusement park in Iowa, the largest at one time. Crowds of up to 4000 would swarm there on weekends.

From the south, people encountered Dexfield hill, the steepest in Dallas County. A Model-T filled with people, its gravity-fed gas tank in the back, easily motored downhill to the park. But returning uphill proved tricky, especially at night. Sometimes they'd have to back up the steep slope, with the headlights shining down the road behind them.

At the entrance, a long lane led to the box office. Admission was $2 for a car, nine cents per person plus a War Tax of one cent.

"Did you know that your folks came here before we were married?" Leora asked the youngsters. "Your dad courted me when I stayed with my Grandmother Jordan at Monteith. That's where we first met. He came for me driving a horse and buggy to spend the day at Dexfield Park. It commenced sprinkling while we were here. The roads were mud in those days, so we had to leave in a hurry." They knew those dirt roads would quickly turn into quagmires.

Dexfield Park, 1918 (Photo: Dexter Historical Museum)

After parking among rows and rows of automobiles, the family could smell popcorn as they strolled to the huge pool to watch the swimmers. Leora had made dotted swiss dresses for her daughters—red for Darlene, blue for Doris. People commented how nice they looked. A row of drinking fountains flanked an Olympic-sized cement swimming pool, which was fed by Marshall's Spring. Swimmers rented towels and suits at a large bathhouse. On special days, an expert demonstrated dives from the top of the tower. The 65-acre park offered a merry-go-round, food vendors, and several other entertainments which caught the eye of the youngsters. Doris could hardly wait for permission to climb the hill to watch the skaters at the outdoor roller rink with a wooden floor.

What a wonderful day to get away from the farm and chores, and the landlord.

The landlady had phoned to inform Mrs. Wilson that they were not welcome to any of the apples or walnuts on the place, that those belonged to themselves.

Once when she'd called to complain about something, an exasperated Leora hung up on her. Several people were on their "party line" and could take down the receiver and hear someone else's conversation. A neighbor stopped by later. "Leora, it's about time someone hung up on that old complainer. I was listening in. She's mean enough to drown baby kittens."

The Wilsons decided that the time had come to move on. If no farm was available for Clabe to run, surely he could always hire out for work, unless other farmers still struggled with debt.

Clabe gave the landlord notice that they planned to move to town, and he asked for his tools back. He never did get them all, and he had to clean the ones that were returned.

The morning they moved, the landlady came to milk the cows. When she left, she wired the wooden gate in such a way that it would be hard for Clabe to open it.

For some reason, she was openly spiteful. Working for this landlord had certainly been a mistake.

◆

CHAPTER 5

Acreage at the Edge of Dexter

By the time school commenced again the fall of 1927, the Wilsons had hauled all their belongings to an acreage on the south edge of Dexter, south of the railroad tracks in the area shown on the old town map as M. J. Marshall's Addition.

The Goffs, who lived north of them several blocks, helped with the younger kids and the moving. Chickens, houseplants, bedsteads and springs, table and chairs, cast iron cookstove, heating stove, kitchen sink, rocking chairs, Leora's precious sewing machine, the Victrola, the washing machine, Mason jars filled with fruits and vegetables, Husky, and the milk cow.

The house was set back quite a ways from the street, with an area between it and the road filled with grasses and wildflowers, including bluebells. Clabe hung the velvet Home Sweet Home picture, the plate rail and their familiar family photos. Leora's houseplants had spent the summer outdoors, but it was time to begin moving them inside to nestle near the windows.

Neither Clabe nor Leora had completed high school, so that became a main goal—diplomas for their children. Leora, the oldest in the family of ten siblings, had asked to go on with her studies, but her father insisted she stay home and help her mother with housework. In fact, Sherd Goff wouldn't allow any of his older children to go to high school. Only the youngest two earned diplomas.

It was a six or seven block walk to school, across railroad tracks, through two blocks of brick stores and businesses on the town's main street, and across the unpaved highway through town. This was a new experience for the Wilson kids. The family had to get used to the rumble and haunting whistle of steam trains. And the town's siren which sounded every day to mark twelve o'clock noon.

Husky trotted along with his kids to the big two-story brick schoolhouse, which held classes from first grade through high school. Seventh graders Delbert and Donald attended classes on the second floor, where the high school also assembled. They took their dinners to school or walked all the way home when they heard the noon whistle. Leora's cinnamon rolls were a big hit with Delbert's friends. He always traded his to Wyman Maulsby for an apple or grapes.

Public School, Dexter, Iowa, 1930

Clabe milked the cow twice a day and hired out to pick corn for three cents a bushel. Delbert and Donald were old enough to help on weekends. From old overalls, Leora made two-thumbed mittens for picking corn. When one thumb wore out, they turned the mitten around. She also made flannel-lined two-thumbed mittens for each child. Leora's busy days included churning butter from the cream she skimmed from their cow's milk. Butter was something she could sell or trade.

Because of the draftiness upstairs and an increased risk of fire in the winter, they carried all the kids' wrought iron beds down to the living room, one in each corner. Clabe and Leora's more modern brass bed sat in a smaller room. The kitchen stove helped keep them warmer.

Dexter, which had been named for a famous race-horse, had three churches in those days—Lutheran, Methodist, and Presbyterian. Goffs attended the Methodist church, which sat a couple of blocks south of their house, so the Wilson children walked there too. After Sunday School all of them paraded to Grandmother's to read the Sunday funnies in the Des Moines paper, especially the *Katzenjammer Kids* and *Popeye*.

By the end of 1927, the Wilson family was blessed with extended family nearby, all seven siblings thriving, and such a good school. The superintendent, Wesley Clampitt, knew Clabe as they'd both gone to the rural Guthrie County school called Frog Pond.

CHAPTER 6

◆

Clabe's Stories

Clabe turned 40 on January 7, 1928. He'd caught a bad cold which just seemed to last and last. He spent part of his sunny and mild birthday sitting with his boys on the cellar door against the house to get some sun.

Back: Delbert, Clabe, and Donald.
Front: Danny, Junior, Dale. January 7, 1928, Dexter

"Dad," said Donald, "Tell us about when you were the nightwatch in Stuart."

"I remember that." Delbert patted Husky, who offered him a paw. "That was about the time Dale and Darlene were born."

The boys settled in. They knew their dad's stories by heart but enjoyed listening to his sonorous voice spinning them once again.

21

Clabe took a draw on his cigarette, then exhaled. "It *was* about the time they were born, when we lived in the Chittick house. Mr. Myers, the nightwatchman before me, got shot when some men tried to rob the bank. After he died, another man and I were hired."

"Weren't you scared?" Donald squinted up at his dad.

"I was a little nervous, but I carried a shotgun and knew how to use a handgun. Do you remember how Jack Beatty's German Shepherd used to go with me?"

"Yeah, Husky," said Delbert. "We'd watch you walk up the street with him when you went to work."

"I'd send Husky to check down alleys for me. He was a real help."

"Tell about when we got our dog just like him."

"Well, when we moved to the farm, I didn't need the handgun anymore. You boys missed Husky and asked if we could get our own dog. When I found a pup advertised in the newspaper I wrote the man, said I'd trade the gun for the pup. He agreed."

"Husky came on the train, didn't he?" Husky perked up like he knew Delbert talked about him. "He looked just like Beatty's dog, dark muzzle and light cheeks, those dark triangles around his eyes. He was so cute."

"Is that why we named him Husky?" Dale twisted back toward his dad.

"Sure is."

Donald shaded his eyes. "Did they ever catch those bad guys?"

"Two men were arrested. I took the train to Guthrie for the trial, but they both ended up getting off."

"So they got away with it, didn't they?"

"Yes, I reckon so. Boys, you're going to find out that life isn't always fair."

That spring Leora bought day-old Leghorn chicks from Pop Scott's, for fried chicken and for eggs to eat and sell. The family planted lettuce, spinach, onions, green beans, bushels of tomatoes, and the nicest cabbage they'd ever raised. They poured suds water from the family wash over the cabbage plants to ward off worms.

They sold some of the cabbage to a local grocer, and also made sauerkraut in ten-gallon stone jars. To make kraut, Leora would chop the cabbage and put it in salt brine. Boards Clabe had cut to fit into the tops of crocks and weighted them with bricks to keep the cabbage under the brine. Leora canned other fruits and vegetables all summer in dozens of glass Ball Mason jars with rubber seals inside zinc lids.

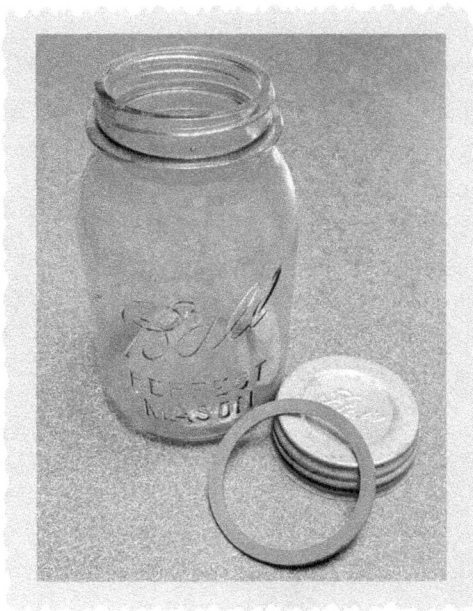

A Mason jar with zinc lid and rubber seal

Leora also made pickles from ripe cucumbers. She'd split the big yellow cukes while Doris scooped out seeds with a spoon. Mother and daughter wore aprons at work. Donald, a couple of years older than Doris, teased her by pulling her apron ties loose while she washed dishes. The next time he did it, Doris swirled around and hurled a soggy dishrag, hitting him in the mouth. That made him mad and he darted toward her. Leora stopped him. "Why Donald, you deserved it!"

Once Doris caught a baby mouse and brought it to the house to show. Donald wanted to see it, but he squeezed her hand with the mouse in it, causing tears. He was not the only older brother to become a pest. Delbert found Doris's 5-cent notebook with names listed of boys she liked. Delbert read it at the dinner table. It was a hard summer to be Doris. Their mother said her older brothers should know better.

Flour and other goods came in printed cotton sacks about 36 inches by 44 inches. In those days, people could not afford to waste anything, especially made of cloth. Women picked out the prints they wanted, trying to get enough flour sacks alike to make a dress. Leora sewed a short dress for Darlene with flowered pantaloons out of a cute print. A lot of flour sacks ended up as aprons, and also bed comforters with worn-out flannel sheets sandwiched between and tied in layers for warmth.

Darlene in a flour sack dress and pantaloons

That August, Herbert Hoover, the Secretary of Commerce and an engineer with major accomplishments was nominated as the Republican candidate for President. His acceptance speech included this hope, "We have not reached the goal, but given a chance to go forward with the policies of the last eight years, and we shall soon, with the help of God, be within sight of the day when poverty will be banished from the nation."

But as poverty had begun to threaten farm communities, Clabe found it harder to find work even during harvest time.

CHAPTER 7

◈

The Cow Dries Up

A son of Clabe's wasn't allowed to carry a gun for hunting until they turned twelve. That important birthday for Donald arrived in September. He had to demonstrate that he could carry it safely over a fence. Clabe was strict about it.

When the six oldest siblings hiked to school in September, Danny started first grade. Junior was the only one at home all day. That fall those eighth-grade boys bought a crystal radio set which came with headphones. The whole family took turns listening to the *Cliquot Club Eskimos*, sponsored by the Cliquot Club soft drink. Leora listened to music with the headphones on while mending socks or patching overalls.

Delbert and Donald watched the high schoolers practice football after school. Superintendent Clampitt asked if they'd like to play with the team. Sure! Clabe and Leora said okay, so they made a trip to the doctor for physicals, and found football shoes they could afford. Mr. Campitt helped them pick out uniforms. Both wore the smallest he had, but it was still way too large for Donald. The brothers were thrilled to get some playing time as substitutes.

The Wilsons began "scraping the bottom of the barrel." When the cow gave no more milk, Clabe sold it for $75.

He and Leora made out an order to Sears Roebuck & Co. They ordered food in bulk—oatmeal, 3 gallons of sorghum, graham and white crackers, prunes, large jars of peanut butter, clothes, boots, winter coats for the kids. Clabe mixed Karo molasses with peanut butter to spread on bread. Sorghum was considered a tonic.

Leora asked Doris if she'd like to choose fabric for a new nightgown. Later, right before Christmas, Doris noticed a box with a broken corner under her folks' bed. A shiny zeppelin peeked through. The wind-up pull toy showed up in Junior's Christmas stocking. "Santa" also left two small boxes on each chair around the table—one with nuts, the other with candy. Doris had suspicions about Santa anyway, then Santa brought her a nightgown made of the fabric she'd picked out in the catalog.

Farm jobs had dried up along with their cow. The Wilsons had no need for the pasture, so they looked for a cheaper place to live. Bleak days of winter were upon them. That $75 was their last cash. Much of it was gone, but spent on things they really needed.

Leora was in a family way again, with a baby due soon.

CHAPTER 8

$$\diamond$$

Whooping Cough

One icy morning in January, Leora asked Clabe to take the five younger children to her folks' house. And to summon her mother. The baby was on its way. Leora's younger sister Ruby Goff minded the Wilson youngsters while they played with their cousins, Maxine and Merrill, who also lived there with their widowed father.

Delbert and Donald stayed with their dad, repairing traps for the rest of the winter and cleaning their guns. While they talked about having a new baby in the family, their frosty breaths hovered in the air. So did Husky's as he snuffled around, keeping them company.

Nearer the time for the birth, Grandmother sent Clabe for the doctor. The baby turned out to be their second set of twins. They looked a lot like Darlene and Dale as newborns—dark-haired and darling.

When Jack and Jean were about three weeks old, the family moved to a drab green house, on the street just south of the Goffs' home.

Grandpa and the uncles, with their gravel truck, hauled the white iron bedsteads, table and chairs, the cookstove, heating stove, treadle sewing machine, the Victrola, pots and pans, curtains and covers. . . . load after load. Leora periodically stopped scrubbing and packing in order to sit long enough to nurse the twins. It was their third move in three years.

Right away Clabe set up the stove in the new house and laid a fire, so it would be warm when the youngest ones arrived. A few at a time rode in the Model T and the truck, along with flowerpots of house plants, and boxes of Mason jars filled with green beans, tomatoes, apples, whatever Leora had been able to preserve.

All nine children, even the babies, came down with colds. It was not long before their coughs grew serious, with a deep tell-tale croup. A doctor confirmed indeed they all had whooping cough. A quarantine sign was posted on the front door, as whooping cough spreads very easily.

Clabe and Leora strewed newspapers upstairs on the wooden floors beside the beds, with ashes in the center to catch the phlegm when they vomited. Short of breath, the kids would fall to their knees from coughing so hard, then gasp for breath. Donald fainted during a coughing episode. Newspapers covered the downstairs floors too. What a miserable time for the entire family.

Every morning, Clabe gathered up those stench-filled newspapers, to burn in the stove, and arranged fresh ones. Every few days, Leora sent the children upstairs to snuggle in bed under blankets to stay warm while she aired out the house, scoured everything, and mopped the floors with disinfectant.

When the stove warmed up the kitchen again, she called the youngsters to come down. The room smelled so clean and medicine-y. Darlene crouched behind the woodstove where she felt warm and safe.

Dale developed pneumonia, a common complication. One night Clabe heard scuffling and squeaking of bedsprings overhead. His oil lamp cast eerie shadows in the stairway as he carried it. He found Dale nearly unconscious, with his head caught in the curves of the wrought iron headboard. The boy was too weak in the disheveled bed to free himself.

Clabe went for the doctor, who brought his bag with a stethoscope, bandages, and medicines. He left medicine for Dale and also checked Doris's bloodshot eye. She'd coughed so hard that a blood vessel broke. The doctor prescribed eye drops, probably boric acid.

Those baby twins gasped and cried. They choked when Leora

tried to nurse them. The harried parents held them upside down, using fingers to work phlegm from their tiny mouths. So that Clabe and Leora could get some sleep, her brother Jennings Goff came over at night to help. He'd already had the whooping cough.

Pertussis, or whooping cough, is most dangerous in infants. The doctor suggested spooning a little whiskey down their throats to try to clear them. But it didn't do any good.

Baby Jack died, then two days later, so did Jean. They were five weeks old.

Grandmother sewed white satin and lace gowns for them. The funeral service, conducted by Rev. Corrie from their church, was held at home in the living room. The seven surviving children sat in another room, with pails nearby, just in case.

The local newspaper noted that the school had sent a bouquet, and so had the Rebekah Lodge, of which Grandmother was a member. Neighbors had taken up a collection for flowers. Carnations. The spicy scent of carnations forever after would take Doris back to the funeral for the baby twins.

TWIN BABIES DIE

The infant twins of Mr. and Mrs. Clabe Wilson, born five weeks ago, succumbed this week to the ravages of whooping cough, little Jack dying on Sunday and little Jean dying Tuesday. The funeral services were held today at ten o'clock from the home, Rev. C. M. Corrie having charge. The little bodies were laid to rest in the Guthrie Center cemetery. In this great grief, the Wilson family has the common sympathy of all.

CARD OF THANKS

We wish to acknowledge with sincere thanks the kindness and sympathy shown us by neighbors, relatives, and friends at the sickness and death of our dear little ones.

The floral tributes from the school, Rebekah Lodge, and friends were deeply appreciated.

Mr. and Mrs. Clabe Wilson.
Brothers and Sisters.

When Leora's younger sister Georgia had died while Goffs still lived in Guthrie Center, her father bought a burial plot large enough for several family members. Two years later, Jennings's young wife

Tessie died of the mumps four days after Merrill's. She was buried in the family plot in 1924. The twin babies' graves were nearby.

After helping Leora burn all the soiled newspapers, carry water, and keep wood chopped for the stoves, Clabe eventually nailed up the plate rail and hung the velvet Home Sweet Home.

"There's been a lot of junky people who have lived in your house," a gossipy neighbor girl later confided to Doris. The shabby house had peeling paint and bare pine floorboards, but it was not so far to walk to school. It was also near their grandparents and cousins Maxine and Merrill, and it gave the family shelter.

CHAPTER 9

◆

Decoration Day

Whooping cough can last several weeks. Delbert and Donald missed an entire grading period at school. Their teachers talked about holding them back a year, but they wanted to graduate eighth grade with their classmates. If they'd double down on their studies and take a special test, the school would allow them to graduate. Which they did.

The Wilson brothers were the only boys not wearing long pants to their 1929 graduation. They wore the same knickers as in the family photos two years earlier, the one in which Danny was yawning.

"Retained in first grade." The heartbroken Danny had been warned that if he didn't get busy in school, he'd have to take first grade again. Leora consoled him with the notion that cousin Merrill would be in his room that fall.

"Mom, I need a white dress for Decoration Day." Girls Doris's age would take part in a ceremony.

"That's dandy, Doris. I reckon I've told you about when I took part as a girl."

"I don't remember."

"The whole town of Guthrie came. Let's see if we can find a dress to fit you. Maybe Grandmother has something to suit."

They walked through the yard toward Grandmother's back door. "We girls rode on a decorated hay rack wagon pulled by a team of Palominos. Will you need a sash?"

"Someone is making them for us, all alike."

"Veterans in those days were from the Spanish-American War and the Civil War. They marched behind us to the cemetery and then helped us lay flowers on the graves."

Grandmother had a white dress that would work. Leora altered it to fit.

Decoration Day was always May 30, no matter what day of the week it fell on. The parade gathered at the schoolhouse. From there, the band led south through town as far as Marshall Street went, then west to the road heading south again to the cemetery. Uniformed veterans followed the band, then the girls in white with red and blue sashes, two by two.

A crowd waited for them at the cemetery. Women with a flower-filled cart handed each girl two clusters of mostly pale blue iris, one to carry in each arm. As someone from the American Legion called out a name of a fallen soldier, a girl laid flowers on his grave. Another name, her other bouquet. Her partner performed the ritual next. The crowd followed through the rows of stones.

After a Legionnaire gave a solemn speech, a trumpet sounded Taps.

Decoration Day parade on Marshall Street

Eighth-grade graduation and Decoration Day. Two ceremonies of normalcy after weeks of whooping cough and deaths. Two sons with diplomas, a large garden planted already yielding rhubarb, greens, and onions. Soon strawberries would ripen in time for Delbert's fourteenth birthday.

The family would be okay.

CHAPTER 10

Husky and the Pack of Dogs

Doris watched a neighbor girl clatter by on the sidewalk wearing roller skates. Would Doris like to try? Sure! The girl showed how to clamp a skate, mainly a flat metal strip with metal wheels, to the thick soles of her leather shoe. Pulling a special key from a string around her neck, the girl tightened the clamp to stay snug. Both girls scooted down the sidewalk with just one skate.

Doris begged until she finally got a pair of her own. About twenty town kids on skates would gather at the Methodist Church, just south of the Wilsons' home. They knew every cracked sidewalk, every chunk of concrete buckled by a protruding tree root, where everyone lived, who had the buckeye tree in their yard, and where each dog belonged. They all knew that Husky was the Wilsons' pet. Sometimes he'd bark and run along with the skaters as they clacked along the sidewalks.

When Leora sent Doris to the post office to ask for the mail, she'd wear them to scurry uptown, tip toeing on the post office's wooden floor. "Get those skates off!" ordered the postmaster. "No skates in here."

Leora and Grandmother, and whichever kids wanted to go along with them, always wore their best clothes when they attended church. Cardboard fans, cut in nice shapes, accompanied hymnals in racks on the backs of the pews. They had stories from the Bible pictured on them. Rev. Corrie was the minister.

Doris played with Evelyn Corrie, the minister's daughter, who wrote plays for the neighborhood kids to act out. Evelyn always starred. Rev. Corrie invited kids to the church every Wednesday to play volleyball or croquet. He was also a Scout leader for a group of boys, which included Delbert and Donald.

Dexter Methodist Church, 1931

A huge mulberry tree grew in the pasture behind the Wilsons' house. Delbert would fix popcorn to take with a book up into the tree. They'd nailed boards on the trunk to use like the rungs on a ladder. Each kid had his own special place to sit, and small platforms fastened in places to make seating more comfortable.

When finished, Delbert used his Tarzan technique of grabbing a branch and swinging to the ground.

The Wilsons gathered and preserved anything they could. When time came to harvest mulberries, Leora had the kids lay old sheets on the ground under the tree. Delbert's specialty was climbing up to shake the tree, causing the ripe berries to fall. Leora canned mulberries with the last of the rhubarb stalks from the garden to have enough for all of them to get through the winter.

Darlene made the rounds of three neighborhood women. She played Nellie Neal's upright piano, even if no one was home.

She listened to Mrs. Wilt tell stories in her German brogue about the old country. And dear Mrs. Bruff Hill allowed Darlene to unpin her hair and brush it.

"Don't be bothering the neighbors," Leora warned.

"But they like me to visit," Darlene said.

"Well, don't go in their houses when they're not at home. That's trespassing. Wait until you're invited."

"Zedonna Neal let me hold baby Rawson the other day." Zedonna was the daughter-in-law of O.S. and Nellie Neal.

"You're eight, Darlene, so you're old enough. Did you enjoy that?"

"I sure did."

"Maybe one of these days you can make some money helping with youngsters."

"I'd like that. Then I can buy candy and things."

Clabe heard that a pack of dogs had been running in rural areas at night, killing a farmer's sheep. Crushed to learn that Husky was one of the suspects, Clabe caught their pet leaving after bedtime. He followed and discovered their pet's tracks headed out to the sheep farm. Back home, he told Leora he'd have to pay for the dead sheep. They just did not have money to throw away, and once a dog started killing, there was only one way to stop it.

While the kids were at school, Clabe took Husky to a remote area where he shot and buried the family pet. How hard to have to break the news to the kids. It shattered all of them.

During sultry evenings, the family took kitchen chairs outside to cool off in the yard. The barefoot kids usually sat in the grass, where they'd watch clouds and heat lightning all around and talk about the universe, wondering how it got started and how it all worked.

Family stories made these evenings more memorable.

"Dad, tell us about your grandfather and the Indians," one of the kids would urge.

Clabe's great grandfather had come to America from Ireland with two brothers. He married in New York State, where his son Sam

Wilson was born. Later the family moved to Sandusky County, Ohio, where this story takes place.

"Well, when my grandpa Sam Wilson was small some Indians tried to steal him. His father found him in a wagon between two Indians, pointed his gun at them, and ordered, 'You let that boy down.' They did." Clabe's cigarette glowed in the dark.

"But when Sam's father died, my grandfather was only nine—about Dale and Darlene's age—but he became an apprentice to a blacksmith. That was back in Ohio. The smith's wife was so mean to him that Sam ran away and ended up living with Indians. He grew up with them."

"Wasn't he scared of them?"

"I guess not. A lot of Indians kidnapped white children when one of their own had died, to replace the missing one. This Sam Wilson moved with the tribe to Illinois where Chicago is now. It was only a fort then."

"I thought you said that during the winter you skated up the river to his place. Did he move to Iowa?"

"He sure did. He married an Illinois girl and they came to Coon Rapids. He acted as an Indian agent in Nebraska for a while, but he came back to Iowa."

Stories helped the family forget the sweltering Iowa weather, gathered in the yard after the hot sun had gone to bed. Enveloped by buzzing tree frogs and blinking fireflies, the Wilson flock relaxed together under Polaris, the Big Dipper, and the Milky Way Galaxy.

CHAPTER 11

Paving of the Great White Way

After long summer days of helping in the garden and mowing yards, the boys explored the road north of Grandmother's house. Butterflies darted along dusty ditches lined with goldenrod, cattails, carroty Queen Anne's Lace, and elderberry bushes. They even found a catbird's nest snuggled among brambles.

When school started that September, the brothers wore their best bib overalls and button shirts with rolled-up sleeves. The younger boys wore hand-me downs, a lighter shade from being washed so many times. Shrubs along the sidewalk wore webs of orb weavers, beaded with early morning dew. Merrill trekked to school for the first time with the Wilson boys, while Maxine accompanied their sisters.

As freshmen that autumn, Delbert and Donald became the first in the family to attend high school.

Washing every Monday was an all-day job. Clabe hauled water from the pump outside, which Leora heated on the big iron cookstove. Clabe hefted the heated water to the wash machine on the back porch, while Leora added a big pot of softened beans and water to simmer all morning on the stove. The school children looked forward to Mondays when the noon whistle signaled that they could head home for ham and beans poured over biscuits.

Leora added shaved clean-smelling Fels-Naptha soap, then loaded bedding and other white things first. After rocking the wooden agitator on the top of the machine for a time, she fed the fabrics through a double roller with one hand while cranking it with the other, wringing soapy water back into the wash machine. Later, a gas-powered wringer simplified that job. While the whites soaked in rinse water, the pile of shirts and dresses and aprons washed next, using the same soapy water. The heavy dark soiled overalls were last.

After using the wringer on the first batch, Leora carried the heavy washing outside to the clothesline. If Clabe was idle, he lugged the wet loads, teaching his boys by example. They used the final water to scrub the back porch and also the cement steps. Any soapy water still left was poured over the cabbage during gardening season to ward off pests.

The Great White Way, also known as White Pole Road, was America's early attempt to create a better road across the nation for growing streams of automobiles. It stretched right in front of the Goffs' home. To make it easier to follow, the poles along the mostly-dirt road were painted white. In the fall of 1929, the paving of the highway was underway.

Grandpa Goff got a job of pulling a wooden drag with a team of horses to smooth the roadbed ahead of the paving machine.

Eastman Kodak camera company gave free Brownie cameras to two sixth graders in area schools. Doris got one of them. She took pictures of the paving going on right in front of her grandparents' house.

Watching the paving rig along the White Pole Road in front of the Goff home, autumn 1929, Dexter.

That fall Clabe took his three older boys to gather black walnuts around where he grew up in Guthrie County. Near Dale City, where some of his older kin had lived, Clabe pointed out a barn he'd helped build as a young man. It was put together with oak pegs instead of nails. While hiking up a hillside, where he said he'd once come upon a den of skunks in his younger years, they stirred up a rattlesnake. Donald, in his haste to jump out of its way, lost his hatchet there, a Christmas gift from two years earlier.

Since black walnuts stain so badly, the gatherers wore old gloves to collect them from under the trees. Clabe and the boys brought home a burlap gunny sack full and spread them in the driveway to dry. A yellow-green husk covers the tough and wrinkled walnut shells and needs to come off. Later Clabe drove over them to help shuck off the outside, leaving the hard shells. Black walnuts are full of protein and have a sharp distinctive taste. Cracking them with metal pincers to get at the nutmeats, the Wilsons enjoyed them all winter long.

The newspapers made it sound like the crash of the stock market that October was a big deal, that most Americans were upset because of it. But the Wilsons' lives did not change at all. Like so many families, they already lived with scarcity.

Clabe finally got steady work at the Redfield Brick and Tile plant late that fall, carpooling with others from Dexter to the factory, seven miles away. Clabe worked in the kilns, where costly leather gloves often wore out, and the intense heat caused painful galling or chafing under his arms.

Meat cost too much, so that's why black walnuts were an important part of their diet. Leora cooked anything her hunters brought home, as long as they skinned and cleaned it first. Clabe taught his sons not to shoot anything they didn't plan to eat, or for pelts they could trade for goods they needed.

Since they had no refrigeration, during the winter up to a dozen or more cleaned rabbits and squirrels hung on the north porch.

Clabe's first check from the tile plant was too late to send a

Christmas order to Sears. All of his kids needed overshoes, but they had to order short rubber galoshes instead of tall buckle ones. Already eleven years old, Doris felt worse for the four younger ones, ages four to eight, than for herself.

CHAPTER 12

◆

1930

The nation's economy worsened and jobs became fewer, but the Dexter Methodist church still managed to hold their Mother-Daughter Banquet that spring. Wearing their best clothes and manners, women and their daughters enjoyed a nice dinner, with a speaker after dessert.

Grandmother Goff took granddaughter Maxine, Darlene went with Leora, and a neighbor invited Doris to be her "daughter" for the evening.

At the banquet, Doris learned that the speaker would be the short plump wife of one of the town's professionals. After the dinner, the eleven-year-old settled back in her chair expecting to be bored. She'd noticed the woman ramble by on the sidewalk wearing moccasins, wrinkled hose, with her slip hanging down from the hem of her dress on one side. "When it was her turn to host DT Club," a neighbor had confided to Leora, "I heard that she served cold boiled potatoes."

Doris was captivated by the woman's presentation at the banquet. She learned an old truism that evening, not to judge a book by its cover.

For Doris, books became an important part of that summer, when Dexter's first public library opened. Townspeople donated a hundred books, shelved in a part of Mr. Percy's law office. Neighborhood girls had talked about *Little Women* so Doris borrowed it first. When she returned it, librarian Una Hemphill asked if she liked it. "Well, I tried reading it three times," Doris confessed. She couldn't relate to the main characters who were from a wealthy family.

"I know some books you might like." Mrs. Hemphill plucked *Anne of Green Gables* from a shelf and stamped the due date slip. Anne was an orphan and poor. Doris loved the story, which was part of a series.

Mrs. Hemphill also recommended Harold Bell Wright books, including *Shepherd of the Hills*. But those "Anne books" became Doris's favorites.

After finishing her kitchen chores, which included ironing shirts and dresses and aprons with a heavy sadiron heated on the kitchen range, Doris spent her free time in the upstairs bedroom she shared with Darlene. She read books in a rocking chair, leaning against the screened window to catch any breeze that sultry summer.

From that reading spot, she overheard their neighbor Nellie Neal tell Leora that her own daughter-in-law, Ruby Neal, had a perfect family of two boys and two girls. News from the clothesline below announced that Ruby was in a family way again. Betty Neal and Doris had just finished seventh grade. What a shock to learn that Betty would be getting a baby brother or sister.

During the school year, cousins Maxine and Merrill lived in the big Goff house. Merrill was in Danny's class in school and Maxine was Darlene's age, so they spent a lot of time together.

Maxine wanted a ring of Doris's so they made a trade. When Grandpa Sherd learned about it, he accused Doris, three years older than Maxine, of sneaky dealing. She should have known better. The trade wasn't an even one, he insisted. Doris did not get a chance to explain her side and ended up in her room in tears.

Another day Maxine came wailing to the Wilsons' kitchen door. "What's wrong, Maxine?" Leora could see that her niece had mighty short hair.

"Grandpa chopped off all my hair!" Maxine swiped at her tears. "I hate it!"

"It looks like he gave you a boybob. It's the new thing, Maxine." Leora barbered for the family, for Clabe as well. "I'll bet Darlene would like her hair cut this new way, wouldn't you, Darlene?"

"Yes, we can be alike." Darlene's dark eyes gleamed.

"Maxine, let me even yours up a bit first." Leora gathered up her scissors and comb, took a chair to the backyard, and set to work. Two nine-year-old girls were soon showing off their twin boybobs.

Wilson and Goff cousins: Danny Wilson, Merrill and Maxine Goff, Delbert (behind) and Doris Wilson with baby Connie Goff. Junior, Donald, Darlene, and Dale Wilson.

CHAPTER 13

$\diamondsuit$

Grandpa's Heart Attack

Sherd had been a fun grandpa when the Wilson children were younger. He made buzzsaw noises with his mouth for the kids, sang a frog song, and stood on his head for them.

But life had not turned out as he'd hoped. Not afraid of hard work, he'd tried making a go of it in the promised land of northeast Nebraska, but "went bust" when the area suffered years of drought. Goffs later emigrated to Key West, Minnesota, with the same results.

Back in Iowa, Sherd had worked his older sons hard. And he insisted that Leora, the oldest, stay home to help her mother. Sherd promised them cash for not being allowed to go to high school, although that did not happen either.

At one time he was known as the "Popcorn King of Guthrie County, Iowa," hauling load after railcar load to market.

Goffs raised enough popcorn to buy a house near Wichita, Iowa. But when the younger sons became old enough for high school, he bought a furnished Victorian house not far from Guthrie Center's big schoolhouse. Sons Willis and Clarence completed high school there, and Clarence even graduated valedictorian.

Sherd bought a commercial crank popcorn machine that you could see through, with a round stainless steel pot. He and his sons sold popcorn at town events.

Sadly, they ended up losing the Victorian house. When the Wilsons moved to a farm near Dexter, the Goff clan moved to Dexter too, taking the popcorn machine with them. The Goffs sold sacks of popcorn on Marshall Street on Saturday nights when the stores stayed open and farmers flocked into town. Soon, grandsons Delbert and Donald helped sack the popcorn.

The machine lasted until one summer when they took it to the Penn Center picnic. It caught fire and was lost.

Grandpa seemed bitter and cantankerous. He spanked Junior, his youngest grandchild, for eating strawberries from their patch. Leora chided her father for scolding a five-year-old. Doris already felt bitter about her grandfather. Now she resented him for his meanness with her little brother.

Sherd hired on to shock oats with Delbert and Donald, in their mid-teens, to show them how it was done. Everyone on the crew wore overalls, long-sleeved shirts against the chaff, and hats to protect from the brutal sun. After making three rounds of the dusty field, all hot and sweaty, they took a water break. Sherd, always in a conversation, stopped talking, became pale, and suddenly crumpled to the ground. He didn't respond when men tried to revive him.

One man ran to his Model T, cranked it to start, and drove onto the bumpy field to take Mr. Goff to the doctor.

"Let's get you boys home," another man said.

Leora and some of the younger kids stooped in the garden with pails picking green beans when a black automobile drove up. Leora stood, watching her sons climb out. Delbert mopped at tears as he neared her. "Oh, Mom." His dark hair was chalky with field debris. "Grandpa took off his hat to wipe his head, not saying a word. He just fell down on the ground."

Leora hugged her shocked sons. "Where is he now? I must see to Grandmother. Boys, shake the chaff from your pantlegs and take these beans in the house for me, will you? I'll be at Grandmother's."

She swabbed sweat from her forehead with the hem of her apron as she hurried to her mother's backdoor. She called for her as the kitchen screen door squealed. She heard voices in the distance, through the house.

The eyes of her ancestors seemed to follow her from the large oval portraits on the wall through the living room.

Grandmother stood at the front door, talking to a man in overalls on the porch. She turned, her hand to her mouth, with stricken eyes. "Oh, Leorie, Pa had a heart attack."

Leora wrapped her mother in her arms, asking the man what he knew. "We took a break and Mr. Goff just collapsed."

"Where is he now?"

"They took him to the doctor, Mrs. Wilson. I'm so sorry, Mrs. Goff, Mrs. Wilson. That's all I know."

Leora's brothers, Jennings and Merl, had been hauling gravel but someone got the news to them that their father had died of a heart attack. They reached town in time to help the undertaker bring the body into the Goff home, where the funeral would be held.

"Oh Pa, Pa!" moaned Grandmother.

Milton Sheridan "Sherd" Goff (1865-1930)

M.S. Goff Obituary
M.S. Goff Died Sunday From Heart Failure -
Had Not Been In Good Health For Many Weeks,
But Death Was Sad Surprise

Sherd Goff died very suddenly last Sunday morning, following a heart attack which came upon him at the Ralph Garland farm just west of Dexter. Mr. Goff had gone to the Garland place to assist in shocking oats. He had labored but a short time when the attack came which caused his death. Mr. Garland discovered him unconscious in the field, placed him in an automobile and hurried him to Dexter, but life was extinct before the doctor's office was reached.

Mr. Goff had enjoyed rugged health until a few months ago. Then an attack of flu with complications enfeebled his heart. For several weeks past he had not been so rugged in health as previously. He was an untiring worker, always engaged in some useful task. It was his natural industry which contributed to his untimely demise.

Mr. Goff was highly respected here, and enjoyed the fellowship of a host of friends. He was a kindly, considerate man, honest and upright. He will be deeply missed by all who knew him.

Milton Sheridan Goff, son of John B. and Florence [I.] Goff, was born July 26, 1865, in Madison County, Iowa. When seven years of age he went with his parents to Cass county near Atlantic where the family resided until he was sixteen years old. His parents next moved to a farm six miles south of Guthrie Center where he grew to manhood.

On February 25, 1890, he was united in marriage to Miss Laura A. Jordan. To this union eleven children were born: Mrs. Leora Wilson of Dexter, Emery [Merl] of Dexter, Wayne of Pasadena, Calif., Georgia (deceased), Jennings of Dexter, Rolla of New York City, Mrs. Ruby B. Blockley of Field Beach, Calif., Willis of Kansas City, Mo., Perry of New York City, Clarence of Omaha, Nebr., and Vernon (deceased).

With the exception of four years residence in Nebraska and two years in Minnesota, Mr. Goff's entire life had been spent in Iowa. For many years he lived on a farm near Guthrie Center. Leaving the farm he moved to Guthrie Center where he resided, with his family, until 1924, when they moved to Dexter, and here had been the family residence ever since.

For twenty-seven years Mr. Goff had been a member of the I.O.O.F. lodge at Guthrie Center.

He leaves to mourn his death his wife, nine children, eleven grandchildren, an aged mother and a brother, Ed, both of whom reside at Miles City, Mont., and a great company of friends.

Funeral services were held Tuesday afternoon, July 22, from the home in Dexter, conducted by the Rev. W. Youtsler of the Dexter Presbyterian church. Interment was made in the Guthrie Center cemetery, the Guthrie Center I.O.O.F. having charge of the graveside committal service.

The Dexter Sentinel, July 1930.

CHAPTER 14

◆

Guilt and Consolation

Leora noticed that her oldest daughter was mopey. "Doris, would you help me snap these beans?"

Doris sat at the table with an enamel pan of them on her lap and began to break the stems off.

Leora also sat, holding her own pan. "It sure seems strange to have Grandpa gone, doesn't it?"

Doris kept her eyes down but said nothing.

"Honey, it's all right to cry."

Doris kept working on the beans. "Mom, can someone die because another person wishes it?"

"Oh, my, no. Where did you get that notion?"

Doris did not answer.

"Do you mean your grandpa?" Leora reached for Doris's hand.

Doris nodded and felt hot tears, her first since Grandpa had died.

"Did you wish he would die?" Doris barely nodded. "Honey, Grandpa was a good man, but he wasn't always nice, was he?"

"Mom, he talked mean to me, he chopped off Maxine's hair and made her cry, and he spanked Junior for the strawberries." She wiped away tears. "Sometimes I hated him. When he spanked Junior, I wished he would die."

"Doris, everybody has some good and some bad in them." Leora began to snap more beans. "Grandpa was just old and crabby. We need to try to remember the good things. You didn't cause him to die. He just had a heart attack from working too hard in the hot sun."

After she had the beans cooking on the stove, Leora asked Doris to set the table for dinner.

"Doris, your grandpa could be a harsh man. He wouldn't allow me to go to high school. That's why I want to make sure all seven of you get your diplomas. But he worked himself just as hard as everyone else. He could have fun too. Remember when he used to stand on his head for you kids?"

"He liked going to the circus with us, and Dexfield Park."

"You know, my father was a man whose life didn't turn out the way he'd hoped."

"What do you mean?"

"He toiled very, very hard all his life. When he married Grandmother, he promised her a beautiful home with all the modern conveniences money could buy. They had so many children and he didn't want her to work so hard. He hoped to give her finer things in life."

"Like the new sweeper?" Sherd had just bought his wife an electric sweeper.

"Yes, Doris. When we all lived in Guthrie County, he bought so many farms on credit that when the prices went down, he lost most of them. It affected us too. Do you remember when we lived in Stuart? We also had to give up our farm."

"You mean the time Dad was the nightwatch?"

"Yes. When we lived there, Grandpa took what money he still had and bought that beautiful Victorian house in Guthrie Center. Doris, do you remember it?"

"I was pretty little, but I remember the red window and curvy staircase."

"That was Grandmother's dream house. But they lost it too before they moved here. Grandpa had worked hard enough to earn his dreams, but sometimes life just doesn't turn out the way you dream."

Since Maxine and Merrill stayed with their maternal grandparents at Wichita during the summer, Grandmother not only missed her husband, she missed having children in the house. The Wilson kids took turns staying with her. When it was Doris's turn,

Grandmother could not sleep because of the monotonous drone of the tree frogs right outside the screened windows.

The heavy oak furniture in her home came from the Victorian house in Guthrie—a large rectangular table and chairs, Mission-style sofa and rocking chair with leather seats, a library table, an oak and glass secretary with knickknacks and a cracked Victorian statue holding a tablet and chalk, like a teacher or student.

Portraits of ancestors hung on two walls in the living room, the Jordans in square ornate gilded frames, Goffs in dark oval wooden frames with convex glass. They made Doris nervous because their eyes followed her.

The Big Dipper hung low in the northern sky in late August. As the sun shifted to the south, the misty dawns began to herald autumn. Elderberries along the north road drooped heavy with dark fruit.

In the fall of 1930, for the first time, all seven Wilson children hiked together to school. Delbert and Donald were sophomores, Doris in seventh grade. It was her first year to climb the wooden stairway to the second floor, where the rows of desks for the upper grades filled the assembly room. Dale and Darlene were in fourth, Danny in second, and Junior started first grade since there was no kindergarten in those days.

Junior's first day of first grade, 1930

Junior wore new dark overalls with deep cuffs, his sleeves rolled up just like the big boys. Leora posed him, clasping a book, in front of a burning bush and sunflowers, for his very first day of school.

1930 - Doris is third from left in the back row.
Dale is in the center of the middle row.

Darlene is second from left in the second row, Maxine is at the right in the same row. Danny and Merrill are in the middle in front.

Mary Drew was in Dale and Darlene's class. Mary's mother, Helen, had started making black walnut fudge back in 1927, using a recipe from relatives in New England. She and her husband made six trays of it and put up a sign, "Mrs. Drew's Candy Shop," at their home along the highway at the west edge of town. Since then, Mr. and Mrs. Drew had experimented with other kinds of hand-dipped chocolates. For the Christmas of 1930, they made a few pounds of candy, especially for the holiday. Despite these Great Depression years, motorists and truckers began to stop regularly at the candy kitchen.

The Wilson family didn't have money for Christmas chocolates, but Clabe sawed evergreen boughs in the timber and tacked them around the oval doorway between the kitchen and living room. What a wonderful piney smell. Doris and Darlene cut snowflakes and stars from folded paper to decorate the boughs. Soon the evergreens turned brown and crisp. They came down as soon as Christmas was over, but they'd looked festive for a few days.

CHAPTER 15

$\diamondsuit$

Clabe's Surgery

There aren't any Wilson family letters or photos during the early 1930s. Doris's Kodak box camera was free but film cost money, and so did having the film developed.

Though details about their lives are scanty, Leora's weeks were crammed with cooking and cleaning, washing on Mondays and pegging it outside on the clothesline if weather permitted. If it did not, she strung sturdy cord across a room to dry sheets and overalls and everything indoors. As soon as sheets dried, Leora remade all four double beds and one smaller one.

Another day she'd heat heavy sadirons on the big kitchen range, then iron the clothing she'd kept damp for easier ironing. Unless the kids took a cold dinner in a bucket to school, they walked home for dinner.

Whenever she sat down, Leora picked up socks to darn, sheets to patch, and knees of overalls, and anything that needed mending. Surprisingly, this little house had electricity, with bare lightbulbs in the ceilings of a few rooms. Having a radio certainly helped pass the time while mending, but Leora tried not to waste electricity by being the only person listening.

People in this small town shared what they had with the family, to send hand-me-down dresses for the girls, jackets for the boys, even spare curtains. Clabe found some WWI jackets but when Delbert and Donald wore those, they endured catcalls of, "Here comes the army."

They still rented the Hammond house, on the east side of the street, situated behind and south of Grandmother's house. Leora's youngest sister Ruby had married and moved to California, where she lived near two other brothers, Wayne and Willis Goff.

Next door to the Wilsons lived O. S. and Nellie Neal. O. S. kept his cows in Pete Jensen's pasture just north of the highway. He milked them twice a day, bottled the milk, and sold it. Delivering the bottles with a horse and cart, he usually hired one of his own grandchildren to hop out and carry the bottles to the customer's door, bringing back empty ones. Occasionally, Mr. Neal asked Doris if she'd like to earn a nickel, which she always did.

On down the street lived Addie Creswell, then Armstrongs, and south of that was the Methodist parsonage on the corner. Methodist ministers, including the Corries, were moved to another church every three years.

Clabe worked as a tile setter in a kiln at the brickyard at Redfield. Leora fixed him a dinner pail to carry every day. It was hot hard work.

The Redfield Brick and Tile Co., featuring beehive kilns. 1939 photo

That March Clabe underwent surgery, perhaps for hemorrhoids, at King's Daughters Hospital in Perry. Clabe and Leora rode there with Dr. Blanchard.

Back home, Leora mailed Clabe a postcard, hoping he was "commencing to be more comfortable." The boys had helped her with the wash, just like their dad did. Anytime their Clabe was home, he shouldered many of Leora's chores. Junior said for his father to "come home right now," but instead Leora told him to rest easy and get well as fast as he could.

"Mr. Neal said he asked Dr. Blanchard how you got along and he said you stood it fine. The Dr. and I were just 45 min. coming home. I'd like to have stayed with you longer, but had to go when the Dr. did. Expect you hardly knew when we left."

Clabe had lost much blood and ended up with anemia. Grind up raw liver, the doctor advised, mix it in orange juice to try to build up the blood. Clabe lacked strength for a long time and wasn't able to go back to work at the brickyard.

He did odd jobs when he could find them. He had a set of metal "shoe lasts" and tools to work on leather, so he repaired shoes for the family and made shoelaces out of tough whang leather. He ordered slabs of leather from Sears & Roebuck, also shoe nails in order to half-sole shoes and replace rubber heels.

"Shoe Needs at Low Prices" from the 1927 edition of
The Sears, Roebuck Catalogue

In spite of its size, Dexter (population 748 in 1930) had one of the best gymnasiums in the area. Their Community Building, built in 1916, was an impressive elliptical-shaped brick auditorium. The roof was supported only by the outside walls, which left a large open space to hold games and accommodate crowds.

1916 Dexter Community Building, about 1930

The school sponsored winter activities, a godsend for families struggling to feed and clothe their children. The boys' sectional basketball tournament was held at Dexter the first week in March, 1931. Both Delbert and Donald got playing time, and later that month, both attended the athletic banquet.

That summer, one of the uncles drove Grandmother, Doris and Maxine to the Goff reunion. Grandmother took bananas and cut them in half to serve at the potluck. Mostly the kids chose them, and one of them ate so many he got sick. Doris had never tasted a banana before.

She was chagrined that day when Maxine called the Wilsons her "poor relations." After Maxine's mother died, she and little Merrill and their father Jennings lived with his folks in the Victorian house in Guthrie Center. The nice furniture moved with them to Dexter, where they not only had enough to eat and wear, the house had indoor plumbing and a real bathroom. Doris's family lived in a small house with an outhouse, and no running water.

But Doris was really taken aback when Maxine, three years younger, broke the news to her at that reunion that Leora was going to have another baby. In those days, pregnancy was not discussed with children. Doris should have noticed her mother's growing girth, but she hadn't.

The birth of a plump baby girl occurred at home on September 15 while the Wilson siblings attended school. Grandmother assisted, as she'd been each time Leora gave birth. Leora, sensing the truth of Doris's reluctance about another child in the family, asked if she'd like to name her. She was the roundest and most beautiful baby Doris had ever seen. She named her Marilyn Louise and took pleasure in caring for her after school and on weekends.

The doctor warned Leora that her tenth child had a weak heart and probably would not live very long, which she never mentioned to the kids.

◆

CHAPTER 16

The Sheepshed

The autumn of 1931, Clabe took a job as a tenant farmer for Bill Myers, so the family moved a mile or so southeast of town. Once more they hauled bedsteads, bedsprings, mattresses, dressers, a kitchen table, a round table, several chairs, the treadle sewing machine, the kitchen sink, the big iron cookstove, a heavy heating stove, stove pipes, dressers, a radio, oil lamps, hundreds of mostly filled canning jars, good-sized house plants vining out of their pots, all their bedding and clothing, pots and pans and dishes.

Every few hours in the middle of the move, when her newest little one started to fuss, Leora rested while nursing Marilyn. Once everything got settled in the house and Clabe had nailed up the plate rail and hung the velvet Home Sweet Home picture, this place was now home for their family of ten.

A narrow hall stretched along the west side connecting all the rooms. They called it the "sheepshed." As usual, the house had no closets, so they hung clothes on hooks on the walls and folded others in dresser drawers. The dining area became a bedroom, with a double bed for Doris and Darlene in one end, two more double beds for the boys in the other with a small one for Junior. Their parents had a room of their own, with their oval wedding portraits hung on the wall, and a "baby cab" or buggy for Marilyn.

They had no electricity but a wooden crank phone on the wall gave access to the local "party line" with neighbors and to the operator for calls farther away. The house was crowded, but they were all used to making do.

Delbert and Donald, juniors that fall, played football. Doris joined the band, playing a borrowed cornet. The seven kids walked to school, a little over a mile, so they each carried a dinner pail. As soon as they got home from school, they changed out of their school clothes to keep them clean for the next day.

Since they had no use for their electric radio at this place, Delbert sold it to the school for $35. The superintendent let the students in the high school assembly listen to the World Series.

The juniors and seniors had rivalries with their class colors, one class posting their ribbons around town, the other replacing them with their own colors. Delbert climbed the Dexter water tower and tied the junior class colors to the top of it. No senior would climb up to replace them, so they fluttered there until they wore out.

When the kids arrived home on October 6, they learned that baby Marilyn had died. No one told them what the doctor had said until then. It was especially disheartening to Doris, as she'd looked forward to caring for her youngest sister every day after school. The same thing had happened when she was a girl, Leora told them. Grandmother's last baby had been "in delicate health" from birth and lived not quite a year.

Relatives and neighbors gathered at the sheepshead for Marilyn's funeral. The family, along with Grandmother, uncles, and cousins drove to the Guthrie Center cemetery. Marilyn Louise Wilson's grave is near Jack and Jean.

OBITUARY

Marilyn Louise Wilson was born September 15, 1931. And she departed this life Oct. 6, 1931. She was the baby daughter of Mr and Mrs. Clabe Wilson who live just east of Dexter. This family has our love and sympathy. Funeral services were held from the home Wednesday afternoon at two o'clock. Interment was in the Guthrie Center cemetery.

Clipping from the *Dexter Sentinel.*

A few days later, a birth announcement arrived from Leora's youngest sister Ruby in California. Curtis was Robert and Ruby Blockley's first child, born the same day Leora's last baby died.

Because it was such a mild fall, with no frost or freeze until November 9, the Wilsons harvested late vegetables from the garden the former tenants had left—tomatoes, green beans, beets. They dug carrots, canned apples from a nearby farm, and gathered green tomatoes to bring in to ripen. Clabe liked tomatoes the way his mother had served them, with sugar and cream.

During the autumn and winter, Delbert and Donald hiked and hunted with their dad through crisp leaves in wooded areas for squirrels and rabbits to feed the family. They also trapped skunk, muskrat, mink, and a few raccoons for income from the furs, averaging $2 per pelt.

Up at 4:30 even on school days, hearing the calls of owls while toting burlap gunny sacks and lanterns, they'd tramp about five miles, checking traps, collecting what they'd caught, and resetting the traps. They left the skinning and pelt stretching chores until after school.

The Wilson family never had a Christmas tree, but by a window in the hallway that year was a large Jerusalem cherry plant—in perfect Christmas colors. It had shiny green leaves and red cherries. The siblings decorated it with paper ornaments.

CHAPTER 17

$$\diamond$$

Yet Another Move

Although only forty-four years old, Clabe Wilson was no longer physically robust, so full-time farming became too difficult for him to keep up with. He suffered from anemia, as well as discouragement. During this dismal winter, they decided to move back into town. In the spring of 1932, with help from Leora's brothers, the family moved to the house east of Grandmother's along the highway. The kids would enjoy walking to school with their cousins again.

"We sure move a lot." Ten-year-old Darlene carried in a vining house plant. "But I'm so glad to be next door to Grandmother and Maxine!"

"They're glad to have us close again too." Leora pointed to the rest of the plants in an east window. "Nothing like being near family, and all of us healthy."

"My neighbor ladies will be glad to see me again—especially Mrs. Neal, Mrs. Hill, and Mrs. Wilt."

"Darlene, just be sure not to overstay your welcome. Be helpful to them if you can."

"I will. They like me to stop by." Darlene perched her hand on her hip. "And little Rawson's mother likes me to play with him sometimes." Rawson was Nellie Neal's young grandson.

"If you like watching children, maybe it's a way you can make some money this summer."

When Coach Zigler formed track and baseball teams, Delbert and Donald went out for both. They practiced running in Pete Jensen's pasture across the highway. Dale tagged along with them.

Delbert was surprised at how fast his younger brother could run.

Once Dale got into a fight with a bigger kid on the way home from school. Danny and Junior ran ahead to tell their mother. The high schoolers were already home.

"Donald, you go see what's happening." Leora paused, holding a dishtowel. "Danny and Junior, you boys stay here. Donald, make sure it's a fair fight."

A bedraggled Dale came home with Donald. "Mom, it was a fair fight," Don told her, "but the other boy's shirt got torn. His mother is really mad. She even said, 'Mrs. Wilson had better get over here or she's liable to take a trip'."

Leora laughed. "Well, it's been a while since I've been on a trip!" She asked Dale if he was okay. He was, just roughed up a bit.

That episode got around the neighborhood. Next time Mr. Neal saw Leora, he called out, "Mrs. Wilson, I hear you're gonna take a little trip!"

Since Delbert and Donald had no suitable clothes for the junior banquet, they did not want to go. One of the teachers, Miss Oelman, came to the house. She and Leora sat outside on the top step, talking quietly. "They are important members of their class," Miss Oelman said. "If it would be all right with you, I'm sure I can borrow suits for them."

They got to attend.

Clabe and Leora stayed busy putting in a garden and harvesting it that spring and summer. The kids all helped on weekends and all summer when they hadn't been hired by a neighbor, mowing grass or doing other jobs.

Delbert and Donald were seniors that fall and Doris started high school. Darlene and Dale were sixth-graders, Danny fourth, and Junior third. Some youngsters started the semester barefooted, including Danny and Merrill.

1932: Top left: Merrill Goff.
Bottom Right: Danny Wilson. Both barefooted.

Thousands of idle men still plodded from town to town in late 1932, looking for jobs. Others drove up from the Ozarks, attempting to peddle chairs they'd made from twigs.

Americans had given up on President Hoover and wanted a change. They elected Franklin Delano Roosevelt president by a landslide.

CHAPTER 18

◆

First High School Graduates

The Dexter girls' basketball team still played three-court ball that year, with two forwards, two guards, and two centers—one running and one jumping. Designed not to be too strenuous for girls, it was a slow game because the ball had to be thrown through center court each time it headed toward the opposite basket.

Doris had played keep-away with her brothers but she'd never watched a basketball game. Yet Coach Wesley Clampitt named the freshman as the running center for the high school team. Coach Clampitt drove the team to away games, which meant riding in the last car to leave for home. Delbert and Donald arrived before Doris, and had already told their folks that not only had she played in the game, she'd been one of the six starters!

Toward the end of the season, left-handed Doris became one of the forwards, handling the ball a lot more.

Clipping from *The Des Moines Tribune, Sports*, January 1933: "Dexter High Girls Seek First Cage Victory of Season. Although beaten in every game so far this season, Dexter has a scrappy team which has displayed good teamwork, but they are handicapped because of size. Verna Maulsby and Doris Wilson will start as forwards, Ethel Schoonover and Mildred McMullen at centers, and I. G. Hoy and Mary McMenamin at the guard. Wilson, although a freshman, is showing promise and is expected to develop into a fine forward."

"Let me assert my firm belief that the only thing we have to fear is fear itself," was part of Franklin Roosevelt's inaugural address.

Two days later he declared a "bank holiday." Roosevelt began holding radio "fireside chats," to explain to the American people what he planned to do to pull the country out of the mire of the financial dilemma.

By that spring, one-fourth of the nation's population was made up of families with no regular income. That included the Wilson family.

They had not lived in the house east of Grandmother's very long before the owner found a buyer. Thankful that the Lewellan house was empty again, just a couple of houses to the south, the Wilsons asked permission to lug everything across the backyards of the neighbors in between.

Dexter freshman Doris Wilson
The Des Moines Tribune,
January 10, 1933
© USA TODAY NETWORK

As soon as Clabe had hung up the plate rail and the Home Sweet Home, the family was officially settled once more. What a blessing just to be together and to live near extended family.

Delbert and Donald played baseball that spring. One memorable loss was to Van Meter, which had a terrific pitcher named Bob Feller. Coach Zigler called extra practices because of Feller's reputation, but Van Meter beat them badly anyway. "Dutch" Reagan, the future U. S. President, covered that Dexter-Van Meter game over WHO-Radio.

Doris joined the Girl Scouts, although no one could afford uniforms. Della Gowdy, a physical education and social studies teacher, and Genora Cushman, who taught Sunday School and collected news for the paper, led the group. At least once they camped in the old Dance Pavilion at Dexfield Park, which had officially closed because so few could afford to attend. Hiking in the heavily wooded area, the girls gathered white Dutchman's Breeches and fragrant pink Sweet Williams for May Baskets to deliver to elderly Dexterites.

This year, Leora began to realize her long-held goal of high school diplomas for her children. Wearing borrowed suits, the first generation of Wilsons graduated high school that May. The commencement ceremony for Delbert and Donald, with thirteen others, was held in the Dexter Community Building.

Their junior-senior banquet had been held at the high-class Grace Ransom Tearoom in Iowa's capital city. Grace Ransom, who had operated tearooms in New York City and Boston, had opened the one in Des Moines on the second floor above the Walgreen Drug Store at 7th and Locust in 1927. It seated 238 customers and the waitresses wore colonial costumes. Known for its cinnamon rolls and fruit salad, the tearoom was the first restaurant in the city to introduce sherbet in the center of a fruit plate. A memorable place for small-town high schoolers to dine.

1933 Dexter graduates Delbert Wilson and Donald Wilson
First in the family to earn high school diplomas.

Dale and Darlene turned twelve in May, which meant that Dale could carry a gun while hunting. And Darlene had started babysitting for Zedonna Neal, a home economics teacher and daughter-in-law of O.S. and Nellie. Rawson was four years old and Jimmie, not quite one. Darlene knew how to keep boys in line.

One day, Leora wondered aloud how an everyday table knife got broken. "Junior keeps sticking them between the table leaves," Darlene informed her. "He flips them back and forth. I told him to stop, but he won't listen."

Junior heard his sister tattling. "Darlene, you're not the boss of me!"

Each house the Wilsons lived in had a good-sized garden spot. Wrinkled rhubarb leaves emerged at the new place in the spring, about planting time for onion sets and lettuce seed. Clabe and Leora sowed "by the moon," checking for the best dates to plant each crop. *The Old Farmer's Almanac* listed dates but basically, crops that matured below ground were to be planted in the dark of the moon or when on the wane, and crops that ripened above the soil should be planted when the moon was waxing or nearly full. Sprouted potatoes, saved from the year before, were quartered to nestle into the soil on Good Friday, according to *The Almanac*.

The Wilsons' well went dry, so along with helping with the family garden, Delbert and Donald hauled water across the highway from Mrs. Wilt's house, which had a deep well. They also hired out, along with their dad, to work for area farmers who had enough money to pay for help that summer.

CHAPTER 19

Delbert to California

Telegram from Uncle Wayne Goff to Delbert: "Willis and I opening beauty supply July first; get you my job $40 month to start; come at once; will wire you money if you need it; will teach you gardening rest of June; room no cost; do own cooking, arrange Donald later; wire collect whether or not."

A job in California! With two uncles to keep an eye out for him. Willis was one of Leora's youngest brothers who'd finished high school and gone on to study chemistry at the University of Iowa. He started a cosmetics business in southern California. Wayne, closer to Leora's age, had not been allowed to attend high school. A veteran of the Great War, Wayne later moved to Pasadena where he had gardening and mowing jobs in the area.

It's hard for a mother to see her firstborn leave home, but Leora helped Delbert pack some clothes and a sack of food for the train. She took a snapshot of him before he boarded the Rock Island at the Dexter depot. The whole family waved and watched the train disappear.

What a long ride for a boy who'd never been out of Iowa, sleeping in the seat. But Uncle Wayne waited for him

Delbert, June 1933
Dexter, ready to leave
for California

at the end of the line. Delbert stayed with Wayne in a small, rented house. Wayne, hauling a push mower and tools in a pickup truck, showed Delbert how each owner wanted their gardens and big lawns kept. Uncle Wayne would get Del started, then drive to Willis' to work with him.

Delbert wrote home regularly. Even though homesick at times but he was often invited to have supper with Uncle Willis and Aunt Ann and their girls, and with Leora's sister Ruby, and her husband and toddler.

While on her rounds of the Dexter neighborhood, Darlene found someone with baby ducklings for sale.

"Mom, can I buy a cute baby duck? It's only a nickel and I'll use my own money."

"Only one? It wouldn't be happy all alone. You'd better buy two."

Darlene used earnings from taking care of the Neal boys. The fluffy ducklings pecked away at anything on the ground. Eight-year-old Danny got so tickled at their antics that he'd laugh until the tears ran. They named them Pick and Pat after a radio comedy team.

Danny with Pick and Pat, a shirtless Junior, and Dale. Dexter 1933

That summer, Clabe worked some in the kilns again at the Redfield Brick and Tile factory. When out of work, he looked for ways to keep busy. Using chunks of small logs, he built a small windmill near the duck pond. Leora planted vines of blue morning glories to climb up the structure, and spicy scented orange nasturtiums to brighten an old tree stump.

Pick and Pat delighted the family as pets during that hot dry spring and summer of 1933. It was so dry that year that nothing grew in the garden, so the ducks couldn't ruin that. The younger Wilsons fixed up a pond in the backyard for them, sinking an old galvanized tub into the ground. The barefoot boys hauled rocks home in a wagon and some evergreen plants, which they called live-forevers, to create a rock garden around the tub. They were right proud of it.

CHAPTER 20

$\diamondsuit$

Bonnie and Clyde

Doris had not camped with the Girl Scouts at Dexfield Park that July. But she learned later that they'd hiked before breakfast one morning. When they came upon a small group of campers, the scouts waved and told them good morning. After returning home, they discovered they'd just encountered the Barrow Gang, commonly known as Bonnie and Clyde.

The five gang members holed up in the park to recover from a Missouri confrontation. Local authorities figured out who they were and rounded up a posse from as far away as Des Moines. A shootout took place July 24. Bonnie and Clyde and their driver escaped.

Officers arrested Clyde's brother Buck and his wife Blanche and took them into Dexter to the doctors' office. Dr. Keith Chapler had started his practice in Dexter just the month before. A tonsillectomy was underway when lawmen arrived abruptly with the outlaws.

Word quickly spread around town. Doris headed toward the doctors' office, along with other neighbors. They watched as a man with a bandaged head and a woman were ushered out of the office, into a car, and driven away. Authorities drove Buck Barrow to King's Daughters Hospital in Perry where bullets were removed from his back, but he died a few days later of the head wounds he'd sustained in Missouri.

The locals had dozens of stories about how long the Barrow Gang must have camped in the park, about how they had been seen in town buying medicine and food, how they always left their Ford running, how they brought the plates back each day and got more food, how one of them bought shirts from night watchman and posse member John Love.

My, had the gangsters driven right by Grandmother's house as they came to town? And shopped right in their stores on Marshall Street? Dexter buzzed with news and gossip for weeks.

Nine months later, Bonnie and Clyde returned to the area to rob the bank at Stuart, the next town west of Dexter. Their crime spree ended in their deaths later in the year.

Scout leader Della Gowdy lived just east of town with her father and blind brother. She hosted a campout of 16-20 girls on their front lawn that August. Each girl was assigned a vegetable to add to a "slumgullion" stew. They were awake much of the night, according to Doris, mesmerized by watching a meteor shower—the mid-August Perseids—and listening to the calls of barred owls, cicadas, and tree frogs.

During the night on another campout in a pasture northwest of town, the girls heard threatening noises from "a bull." They woke Della and everyone ran to escape across a fence. The "bull" was just local cows curious about the humans camping in their field. Someone drove out to take the girls back to town. They piled into and on the automobile. Doris and another girl jounced along standing on one running board, holding onto the car frame through a window, while two others traveled along the dusty rural road on the opposite side.

Since Merrill and Maxine spent their summers with their other grandparents, Grandmother Goff decided to visit her daughter and sons in California for the first time—Ruby, Wayne, and Willis. Delbert had enjoyed his train ride there, and Grandmother, at age 64, wasn't too old to travel alone.

She attended the annual Iowa picnic. The names of Iowa counties tacked to trees in a park helped find people from home to visit with, people who'd moved to southern California. Grandmother had news of several Guthrie County folks she'd visited with.

Iowa picnic in California, 1933—Wayne, Grandmother, Willis, Ruby

From his gardening job, Delbert saved enough to send money home for the kids' schoolbooks and some Prince Albert tobacco for his dad. He mailed a couple of two-dollar bills, hoping they were legitimate. Counterfeit money was in the news. But as the summer of 1933 wore on, even the wealthy Californians began to feel the pinch of the Depression and began to lay off their gardeners, including Delbert.

Willis and Wayne dissolved their partnership. While Wayne hunted for another job, he also showed his mother the Rose Bowl and a big dam. When he took her to stay with Ruby, she got to see the ocean for the first time. She marveled at the big battleships and "airplane carriers." Wayne said if he were young enough, he'd sure join the Navy, which would be better than "this gardenin' job now."

Delbert reluctantly returned to Iowa. Howard Benz, a classmate of Delbert and Donald's, had joined the Navy. Delbert wrote to ask what he thought about the navy.

It's the best thing for a boy to do, he answered, and he'd encourage anyone who could pass the exams to join. He liked it better every day and had gained twenty pounds in just a month. "The training and discipline surely makes a man out of a person." He always had something to look forward to and expected to have $1000 saved when his four years' enlistment was up.

CHAPTER 21

◆

A Biplane Ride
Before School

Mrs. Wilt gave her old pump organ to the Wilson family. Both Doris and Darlene played in the school band. As a girl, Leora rode a horse to town for piano lessons. She'd substituted for the regular pump organ player at their rural church. But these days, Leora was pretty absorbed with all the household chores, and summer meant canning every fruit and vegetable she could so they'd have enough to last until spring.

Clipping, probably from *The Sentinel*:

Champion Gardeners of Dexter Ready for Next Season—
Clabe Wilson Family Has Made Praiseworthy Record in
Producing Food on Small Plot by Genora Cushman

"For real gardening, which takes in the entire gardening season from early spring to late fall, we take off our hats to the Clabe Wilson family. Every inch of their medium-sized garden at the back of their home in Dexter has been utilized for the growing of vegetables during this past season. As soon as one crop was finished, the spot was replanted for another crop. A fall garden brought forth abundantly, after other gardens had been abandoned to weeds. This garden was kept spotlessly clean for weeks throughout the growing months, the boys being largely responsible for this.

"Mrs. Wilson, with the aid of the other members of the family, has canned an unlimited amount of food for the coming unproductive months, from this bit of ground. And now the final harvesting of tomatoes, cabbages and other late vegetables has been completed; the vines and dead foliage have been raked and burned; and the ground is as bare and clean as a tennis court. It is all ready for the plowing in the spring and the starting of another model garden."

That September, only five Wilson kids hiked to school with their cousins. Doris was a sophomore, Dale, Darlene, and Maxine joined her on the second floor of the school as they began seventh grade. Danny and Merrill were fifth graders and Junior was a year behind them.

There was a chill in the air one morning when a small noisy plane drew half the neighbors outside to watch the sky for it. A biplane had landed in a field east of Gowdy's farm and was zooming over the town of Dexter.

Early, before school.

When Dale, Danny, and Junior heard it go over earlier, they got permission to run out east of town to see it.

As the low plane droned overhead, a boy's cap flew out and sailed down onto Leora's tomato patch.

"Well, if that don't beat all!" Leora watched with her neighbor, Addie Creswell. "My boys are up there having a ride!"

"All three?" Addie lived next door.

"Yes!" Leora and Addie both headed for the cap that had landed in the garden. "Those boys ran out to Gowdys'. The pilot said he'd give them a ride for a dollar a piece. You should have heard them counting out all their summer earnings."

"Do you s'pose one of them threw his cap out?" Addie still watched the sky.

"I reckon it was no accident!"

It wasn't long before three breathless boys in overalls had run the mile and a half home.

"Wow, that was fun!" Junior panted. "Where did you find my cap? I threw it out right over the house."

"It landed right in the tomato patch. You'll sure have something to tell at school this morning!"

Danny declared, "Whew! Best day of my life!"

"What a swell ride!" Dale said. "I'd sure like to be a pilot someday."

"You boys get your dinner pails. Hurry! It's about time for school to commence."

After a ride in a biplane before school, how could three boys keep their thoughts on their studies?

Clabe and boys in their parched garden. Dexter, July 22, 1934

October in Iowa is pure bliss as shades of green transform into golds and russets. The soul of autumn, clear blue sky, and crisp dark nights glittered with stars. Sparks of bittersweet and sumac glow along chalky roads. Spikes of cattails line dusty ditches. Goosebumps accompany the autumn aroma of end-of-harvest bonfires.

Delbert and Donald trapped and hunted with their dad. One evening it snowed hard, so they planned to go hunting since tracking prey proved easier after a snowfall. But the next morning, a fine dust coated everything. It was Iowa's first dust storm, November 12, 1934. Hunting was a real mess that day, according to Delbert, but still good for tracking.

Farmers went bankrupt, and some had burned corn for heat. Farms were put up for sheriff's sales, sold to the highest bidder. Men began to organize, carrying their shotguns to the auctions, sending word around not to bid over a nickel so the man would get his place back. A rumor circulated that farmers had kidnapped a judge, who finally tore up the foreclosure orders. People worried.

Pick and Pat had grown so much that they ate everything in sight. Leaves on the vines disappeared higher and higher, leaving naked stems. Every plant within reach became scraggly. The ducks left bigger and bigger messes to clean up. Washing off the sidewalk was a regular chore. Clabe began to call them Pick and Splat.

After the first frost killed the vegetation, the money-strapped family needed to buy feed for them.

Thanksgiving solved the problem. Leora made the best roast duck and dressing Doris ever had in her life. She didn't even shed a tear.

Pick and Pat became a hearty Great Depression era holiday dinner, but only for those Wilson kids who managed to eat former pets.

Squirrel and rabbit were their main sources of protein, but for Leora's forty-fourth birthday, that December 4, the family celebrated with a "nice fat roast coon."

◆

CHAPTER 22

Delbert and Donald Join the Navy

Four million men "on relief" worked at government jobs for paltry wages, mainly working on public roads, but in 1934 it Clabe found it difficult to get hired. Delbert and Donald decided the best thing they could do, for themselves and for the family, was to join the Navy.

Their folks did not like the idea, but times had steadily gotten worse. Joining the Navy beat idleness, they agreed. Boys with nothing to do get into trouble. They'd get enough to eat, learn a trade, and see new places. After asking the brothers to promise not to get tattoos, Clabe signed the papers for them to enlist. Donald was just seventeen.

They cranked up the Model T truck and motored to Des Moines where they signed paperwork to join up. They came home with a new sled for Dale, Danny, and Junior. And a Silvertone radio for the family.

Donald and Delbert Wilson, January 1934, Dexter, Iowa, snowing.
"Grandmother's house" is in the background.

Danny, Junior, and Dale with the new sled. January 1934

Clipping from *The Sentinel*, February 15, 1934:

Wilson Brothers Enlist in Navy

"Donald Woodrow Wilson and Delbert Goff Wilson were enlisted in the Navy at the main station in Des Moines on Feb. 10, 1934, according to information received from Lieut. Com. W. L. Taylor, Officer in charge.

"They are the sons of Mr. and Mrs. Claiborne Wilson, who reside at Dexter, and they are now located at the Naval Training Station at Norfolk, Virginia, for their recruit training which will cover a period of twelve weeks. At the conclusion of this training they will be assigned to a ship of the United States Fleet for further duties, and will in all probability make the return voyage with the Fleet to the West Coast when those ships leave the East Coast area in November.

"Both these boys are graduates of Dexter High School, and they look forward with great anticipation to their prospective naval career."

The brothers were assigned watches, slept in hammocks, learned to wash their own clothes and bedding, and did their own ironing. "Boy do we eat!" one wrote home. They also got shots, studied their Apprentice Seaman book, drilled, had inspections, and marched in formation everywhere— to chow, church, movies, and for ice cream on Sundays.

Finally, enough to eat, worthwhile activities, plus a paycheck. They sent home a little money each month to help "fill the bellies" of five younger siblings and for coal to heat the house.

Clabe's meager part-time job involved roadwork, but at least it paid the rent. The government allowed only fourteen hours a week at 40 cents an hour. He was selected as a teamster to drive mules on a job at Waukee, but he couldn't afford to take the job. It cost too much to carpool 64 miles round trip.

Darlene still looked after eighteen-month-old Jimmy Neal and his older brother. The daily duties of cooking, washing, ironing, mending, and house cleaning kept Leora busy. Doris helped her mother but also had basketball practice and games. And the younger brothers kept the new sled busy.

"The Navy is the one and only place for a fellow," Delbert wrote home. "He is sure of his 3 meals a day and a place to sleep plus travel and pay and a chance to learn a trade. All of this is uncertain in civil life." Donald had already gained weight, from 157 to 175 pounds.

The Navy boys' letters provided family entertainment—news about boat drills, KP duty, and learning to swim. While playing football, they'd found some boys from Casey who'd joined up, and in the chow line, met one from Monteith.

They'd also encountered something new for breakfast—Rice Krispies.

After twelve weeks of training and discussing how they could afford the trip home, Delbert and Donald earned ten days of leave. How good to have the family together again.

When Warren Neal, a Dexter junior, visited his grandparents, O.S. and Nellie, he learned that the Wilson brothers were home.

They'd played football together so Warren stopped by to see how they liked the Navy. Having a visitor in their home that spring day, Doris keenly noticed how sparse their furnishings looked.

After returning to Norfolk, Delbert and Donald received orders to report to the same ship that classmate Howard Benz already served aboard, the cruiser USS *Chicago*. They ran into him about every day.

Donald Wilson, Howard Benz, Delbert Wilson
USS *Chicago*, 1934

The USS *Chicago* - Philadelphia, July 4, 1934

The brothers began to see the world. The *Chicago*, as the flagship of the scouting force, led four destroyers to Philadelphia. "We are having the time of our lives," Delbert wrote. Visitors came aboard every afternoon, and the sailors were allowed shore leave. They marched in an Independence Day parade there, attended church, and visited Independence Hall. Every evening the ships in the harbor put on a searchlight display.

CHAPTER 23

Running the Town Pump

That June Clabe began keeping the Dexter town pump running, a part-time government job which lasted nearly a year. A brick hut housed the machinery on the southwest corner of town, out toward the cemetery. From home, Clabe hiked south to the railroad tracks, followed them as far west as he could, then south again to the pump house. He was hired to work sixteen hours a week.

Iowa had record heat that summer. Over half the country suffered from drought and seared crops. It reached 115 degrees one day. A Dexter classmate, writing to the Navy boys, signed his letter, "Cemetery of Dexter, State of Dried Up Corn."

"I want you to fill the boys and girls up," Donald wrote from Provincetown, Massachusetts, "on some pork chops and mashed taters and gravy and a big glass of milk with some of the money I'm going to send. I think of you when I'm eating chow. How I'd like to have you all eat a Navy meal with us. Junior would sure go for the pie, I bet."

He wanted to know what "all the fellows around town" did for excitement. "As for you, Dad and Mom, I wouldn't worry about the times. We'll get by somehow. Boy, the people all over the country are sure destitute. The condition of the people in Provincetown here shows on their homes and their faces. But worrying over it doesn't do a bit of good.

"I just thought how lucky we were to be able to be in the service. Especially in these times. We are away from home most of the time, but you can't always be at home all your life. We can send money home—that's more than the majority of the men our age in civilian life could even make."

When their ship docked at the New York Navy Yard, Delbert and Donald, along with other young sailors, gaped at the New York skyscrapers, the Brooklyn Bridge, and the Statue of Liberty from the deck of the *Chicago*. The cruiser was docked there long enough that their Uncle Perry Goff visited, then took his nephews on a tour of the city.

Perry and Rolla Goff, Leora's younger brothers, never finished high school and never married. Both "played the horses" in New York and Florida and did hotel and restaurant jobs. After Uncle Perry took his nephews on the subway and up the Empire State Building on a fast elevator, he bought them a fifth of wine for $4 and all the beer they could drink.

Uncle Perry had paid for everything. "What the hell," he told them, "I made 128 bucks on the horses yesterday."

Leora warned her sons not to carry much cash on them. She'd read that a Navy boy was robbed of $110 at Cedar Rapids.

"If it would rain," Leora wrote her sons, "we would have turnips, popcorn, and tomatoes, but we are trying not to worry about it as we just can't do anything about it." Leora wanted to get as much canning done as she could.

Job prospects dwindled as farmers turned away help. No corn husking. Farmers cut fodder before that got too dry. And their garden could use four feet of snow.

Leora and Clabe, Dexter,
July 22, 1934
"Depression! and how! and
dry! Dusty, Wells dry!
gardens burned!"

Restless Clabe wished hunting season were open. He backed the "Struggle Buggy"—what folks called old vehicles—out of the shed for the first time since the brothers had been home on furlough. He trundled to Guthrie County to find wood and ended up in Dale City, where he visited with his aunt, a sister of his mother.

Clabe could see why his ancestors had settled in the richly wooded area. Catbirds mewed along the roads. Blue jays abounded, as did tiny bluebirds and finches. Their songs were accompanied by the squawking of pheasants, frogs croaking, the buzzing and snapping of all sorts of insects. Bur oaks, maples, pines, and hickories grew in abundance, but now the whole territory was "all burned up." Cattle had eaten the brush just as high as they could reach. Teams of horses all along the road hauled water from the river, as the drought had settled in and wells dried up.

CHAPTER 24

$\diamondsuit$

Machine Perm in Redfield

The Wilsons' teenage daughter wanted a permanent wave. The summer before her junior year, Doris heard that a Redfield woman gave machine perms for $3. From babysitting a doctor's children (25 cents an hour if the wife paid her, 50 cents an hour if he did), Doris had saved up the $3.

But how to get the seven miles to Redfield and back? Her mother decided she would go with her and found someone traveling to Redfield. He could not bring them home, but they could start on foot. Surely someone from Dexter would be headed south out of Redfield and give them a ride the rest of the way.

For being out in public, which included attending her daughter's first perm, Leora wore her good dress and shoes with two-inch Cuban heels.

The beautician started Doris's "machine perm" by bathing strands of hair with a chemical solution, then smoothed each section around a metal roller. A clamp secured each one, then cords tethered them to an electrical contraption that heated curlers, solution, and tresses.

Picture Medusa from mythology. Doris's hair began to sizzle.

She kept her head very still. The whole room smelled of strong chemicals. When a spot on her head got too hot, the operator blew on it with small bellows. Every so often the hairdresser unclamped and unrolled a curler to check the progress. When she determined that the curl was complete, she undid the rollers to reveal the new ringlets.

Doris, happy with her new look, counted out the $3, all in coins. "Be sure to wait a week before washing your curls," she was cautioned.

Doris, reeking of chemicals, and her mother headed south out of town on foot. Cars breezed by, swishing their skirts, but no one they knew stopped to offer a ride.

In spite of the hills, they enjoyed a pleasant trek back to Dexter, except for that one big downslope about halfway home. As mother and daughter trudged down the steepness, Leora's feet slid forward in her shoes.

After they got home, Leora sat down and pulled the shoes from her sore feet. Doris was so thrilled with her new waved hair that she did not realize her mother had suffered.

During the next few days, Leora's toenails began to turn black. Eventually, she lost most of them.

Otherwise, the machine perm was a success–no more curling iron before school. It left the ends of Doris's hair a reddish color from being singed, and pieces of her hair broke off for quite a while.

Both Doris and her mother were reminded by the hills south of Redfield that Iowa certainly is not flat.

CHAPTER 25

◆

Rusty the Pet Squirrel

Every September, Leora sent her flock back to school, with reminders to do their best. But boys will be boys.

A schoolmate needed a smoke, so Merrill and Junior went with him, out behind the fifth and sixth-grade building. Both tried smoking. Mr. Clampitt happened to check out the science room window and did not like what he saw. He spanked the boys and warned them not to get caught by the nicotine habit. After school let out, he paid a visit to their parents to let them know what he'd done. They approved.

Once when Clabe had been squirrel hunting, he brought home two young ones in his pockets. They must have been orphaned as they readily came to him. The Wilsons fed them raw oatmeal and milk. "My, the kids sure think lots of them and, of course, Dad does, too," Leora wrote the Navy boys, "and I guess I do, too." Clabe fixed a box for them and they became family entertainment. The bigger one didn't last long, maybe from overeating.

They named the survivor Rusty. He hid nuts and other small things in the door of the sewing machine cabinet. He'd grab the pencil or pen from someone writing a letter, and scamper away with it.

Clipping from *The Sentinel*, Sept. 19, 1934: "Rusty," a recently acquired pet squirrel, is quite the most important member of the Wilson family in Dexter. The boys found the tiny fellow nearly starved, apparently an orphan, so they brought the hungry baby home, fed him bread and milk, and how he has thrived on these rations. He is especially fond of peaches and will also eat all the bread and butter you will offer him. He climbs all over anyone who will pick him up, nosing into pockets and sleeves in search of any hidden crumbs of food. He is quite the cutest pet we have seen in some time."

Clabe and Doris took the Model T truck to gather black walnuts in the timber near Bear Creek. They brought home the load and dried it in the yard before attempting to husk them.

Although Rusty began to spend less time with the family, he showed up when Doris cracked walnuts on the back step and helped himself to the ones she'd already managed to open.

Delbert and Donald's allotment checks helped pay for rent, winter clothes, and a pair of shoes for Leora. "She sure was needing them," Clabe wrote. "Mom and I are sure thankful that we have two boys that will do that."

Clabe pulled off the top of the truck, transforming it into a "sports roadster." Dale, Danny, and Junior all laughed at what he'd done. They took their roadster to get a load of coal. The boys had never seen miners with lamps on their helmets.

Clabe, Dale, Danny, and Junior with the "roadster."
Rusty is on the fender.
Dexter 1934

Coal cost $3.25 per ton, cheaper that fall than wood, which went for $3.50 for a 26-inch load. Clabe also got "government wood," a load of it for a day's work. Work was still hard to find for the thirty-five Dexter men who needed government help. Clabe still pumped water for the town four half days a week.

Clabe bought shells for hunting season, looking forward to having squirrel for supper. "We have one now running around the house all the time," he admitted.

CHAPTER 26

◆

The Panama Canal

That fall, tugs headed the USS *Chicago* out under Brooklyn Bridge, underway to pick up new recruits in Norfolk, then to Cuba to meet the rest of the fleet. "The whole time, etc., of the arrival in here was kept secret. We came in darkened all the way." Delbert wrote all about transiting the Panama Canal, heading to their base at San Pedro, California, and with "war games" exercises on the way.

The Wilsons at home used a map, looking up every place the Navy brothers mentioned. That map enhanced the kids' schoolwork. Junior had just studied the Panama Canal in geography.

November 6 was election day, to "vote for or against the New Deal. We are for it, of course—give the Democrat program a chance to work out rather than go back to the *old deal*. . . . Roosevelt is for a '*Navy second to none*'."

Clabe and Leora listened to a Detroit radio priest, Father Charles Coughlin. In his Irish brogue, he warned against money changers, "subversive socialism," and said that international bankers had ruined America. Each week, he lectured from his Shrine of the Little Flower in Royal Oak, Michigan. "The New Deal is Christ's Deal," he declared, endorsing Roosevelt. He announced the formation of the National Union for Social Justice.

The Wilsons also listened to Upton Sinclair, while the boys played outside with the football Donald had sent them. About twenty boys often played past dark in the pasture across the highway.

Clabe finally sold the old roadster and bought a suit with the money, so he and Leora could "step out a little," he quipped.

Their Thanksgiving dinner consisted of canned government veal, cranberries, cabbage with mayonnaise, potatoes and gravy, celery, and fruitcake. "We are all so thankful we are all well, aren't we?" Leora wrote. "And just a lot of things to be thankful for, not only for one day but for all the days which bring things good."

As soon as the *Chicago* arrived in California, Delbert and Donald got mail from their Aunt Ruby and Uncle Willis, wanting their nephews to visit. The Navy brothers spent Thanksgiving at Aunt Ruby's.

The next allotment paid for a couple of tons of coal from Waukee. "Sure is a blessing to us. Guess you know how thankful we are."

Leora wished she could listen to Father Coughlin on the radio for five hours instead of just one. He railed against capitalists and other cutthroats as the main trouble in the nation. In December, he touted his seven principles to combat capitalism and mass production. He ridiculed bankers and announced his own plan for a $10 billion public works program. He demanded that congress nationalize all money. He saw no hope for modern capitalism or modern democracy in America, insisting that the nation's only salvation was through social justice.

The Wilsons received government meat (frozen veal or canned beef) nearly every week—seven pounds of veal, two cans of beef, and three small blocks of cheese in December and occasionally some butter and rice. They so hoped that Clabe could find work come spring. "That is what people want, you know, to do something for themselves and be independent and live as American citizens should, not just an existence." Father Coughlin said so.

An Old Age Pension group met at the Dexter Community House, with an enthusiastic audience of about 200, according to the newspaper. Clabe and Leora attended. Called the Townsend Plan, a proposed two percent tax would provide a pension of $200 per month to anyone over 60. They'd be required to spend the money within a month to help stimulate the economy.

There was no sound argument against the revolving pension plan, the Secretary of Iowa Crowningshild told the crowd. Now, if only the government would just accept the plan.

◆

CHAPTER 27

A Suspicion Before Christmas

Most area schools, including Dexter, had officially switched from playing three-court girls' basketball to two-court, with three forwards and three guards.

Doris was elected captain. Tiny Dexter beat Guthrie Center, which is a county seat town. The Guthrie coach, a regular at Parrish's Cafe in Guthrie, came in for a meal after they'd lost to Dexter. Embarrassed that they'd been beaten by such a tiny town, she nevertheless mentioned an especially good small forward.

Cora Parrish, who was Grandmother's younger sister, asked, "Was she left-handed? Name Wilson? She's my niece!"

But when Dexter played in Guthrie Center's new auditorium, they lost. The Guthrie girls went on to win a tournament that year.

The coach invited Darlene, then in eighth grade, to practice with the team. Leora could not make it to a basketball game very often, but kids accompanied by a parent got in free, so she went when she could.

Cousin Merrill got a new Flying Arrow sled from Sears. He'd "just yearned and cried for one—his other was a 'gonner,' you know, till Jennings thought he'd better have one. My, he is tickled, just like when you boys got these boys a new sled," Leora wrote.

Merrill let his cousins try it out. Danny came home with rosy cheeks. "My, that's the most fun a boy ever had."

The Wilsons often had wheat for breakfast. "I wash it (after dusting it in the wind) in 3 waters," Leora wrote, "then put in the big flat pan in the oven and dry and brown it a little. And say, it is delicious when cooked. I like it with just butter, no sugar. Now isn't that news? Got to write something, you know."

Leora mailed them a package, "so you'd have just a little from home for Christmas. Doris and I made some—I guess you can tell which kind—the <u>divinity fudge</u> I used to make and you boys used to like so well."

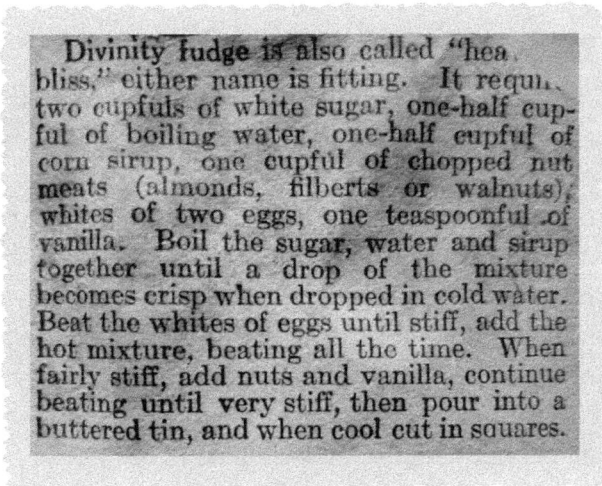

Clipping of the recipe in Leora's small Memorandum book: Divinity fudge is also called "heavenly bliss," either name is fitting.

Railroad officials had asked around town about anyone seen spending time along the railway. It looked like something had been deliberately placed on the tracks to hinder the trains. Clabe Wilson's name came up, and a railroad worker questioned him. Clabe occasionally drank to meanness, but he was honest to a fault. The suspicion stung.

The whole family looked forward to visits from Clarence Goff. He brought his mother a dandy electric mixer from Omaha for Christmas, a box of candy, and an already-dressed turkey. He also brought a box of 'kerchiefs for each of the girls, a football for Merrill, a pound of Prince Albert and some "cough medicine" (alcohol) for Clabe and brothers Jennings and Merl, and candy and nuts for everyone.

Clarence owned a heating and cooling business in Omaha.

Neighbors O. S. and Nellie Neal gave the Wilsons a nice fat hen, which Leora served for Christmas dinner, along with potatoes and gravy, dressing, celery, Danny's favorite cranberry sauce, pickles, fruitcake, and Clabe's favorite lemon pie.

The Christmas of 1934, their Navy boys were blessed with plenty to eat, visits with aunts, uncles, and cousins, and extra income to send home. The younger five siblings thrived, doing well in school and enjoying winter activities.

Both Clabe and Leora came down with grippe, but all in all, things felt more hopeful.

CHAPTER 28

◆

The Imbedded Needle

Clabe trudged along the Rock Island tracks on New Year's Day 1935. He shivered as he headed to the pumphouse, brooding about being suspected of a misdeed. Was it common gossip around Dexter that he could not find a real job? That he sometimes drank too much? Drab smoke drifted from chimneys into the weary winter as he plodded by each house. Clabe sat inside the desolate and cold little brick pumphouse, with nothing to do but keep the pump oiled. Yes, it was shelter but had no heat. Clabe wore long johns all winter, and he bundled up for the half-day shift.

The turkey Clarence gave them for Christmas, which they'd kept frozen on the porch, became New Year's dinner.

The family listened to the radio broadcast of the Rose Bowl game from Pasadena. Uncle Willis tried to purchase tickets but the game was sold out. Uncle Wayne lived in Pasadena, so Delbert and Donald watched the parade, a dozen large bands, and several floats. Wayne also took them to the horse races.

Being on welfare in the 1930s was called being "on the dole" or "on relief." Families were ashamed to accept money and food paid for by other citizens. The Wilsons carried that guilt.

"Continued dependence upon relief," President Roosevelt said in his State of the Union message, "induces a spiritual and moral disintegration fundamentally destructive to the national fiber. To dole out relief in this way is to administer a narcotic, a subtle destroyer of the human spirit. . . . It is in violation of the traditions of America. . . . Work must be found for the able-bodied but destitute

113

workers. The Federal Government must and shall quit this relief business."

But what to do with five million unemployed now on relief? Clabe put his hope in the old-age pension Townsend Plan, saying that when it got passed, "we all can get a job anywhere."

"Well, boys," he wrote, "I know it is hard to save money, but you have a good job, clothes, and plenty to eat and can have a good time on the side. That is better than anything I know of out here in the corn field. If you like your work, that is everything. And you can learn while you are doing it."

In a January photo, Clabe has on his new three-piece suit and a woolen cap. Leora is dressed in a dark two-piece outfit, pumps, silk stockings, and a hat with a little feather. They were not dressed up for a wedding or an outing. They were waiting for a ride to the Adel clinic to have a needle removed from Leora's hand.

Her tub washer broke so she scrubbed the laundry––for seven people––on a corrugated metal washboard. She felt a stab in her hand. She'd forgotten she'd parked her sewing needle in the bib of her apron. It happened so fast. The tip broke off so she could not get a hold of it to pull it out.

They had no extra money for a doctor but, Depression years or not, she needed one.

Dr. Chapler numbed her hand and fished around for the needle but was not able to locate it. He sent her home, said to soak the hand in hot water, and he'd set up x-rays at a clinic for her.

Leora numb hand could not feel how hot the water was and she scalded it. Surgery had to wait until the burn healed.

Then they borrowed Pete Jensen's car to go to Adel again to have it removed. An x-ray pinpointed the fragment of steel, but Dr. Chapler still had trouble finding it. When he managed to cut it out, Clabe said that Leora's hand looked like a piece of meat. Afterwards, ether used as an anesthetic made her nauseous.

Why get all dressed up to have surgery?

During those Depression years, most folks had two sets of clothes. For Clabe, it was overalls and the suit. Leora's choices were a worn-out house dress and her good one.

Porous plaster encased Leora's hand for about a month, so they were thankful that Grandmother was nearby to help Doris with cooking.

Clabe and Leora Wilson
Dexter, January 1935

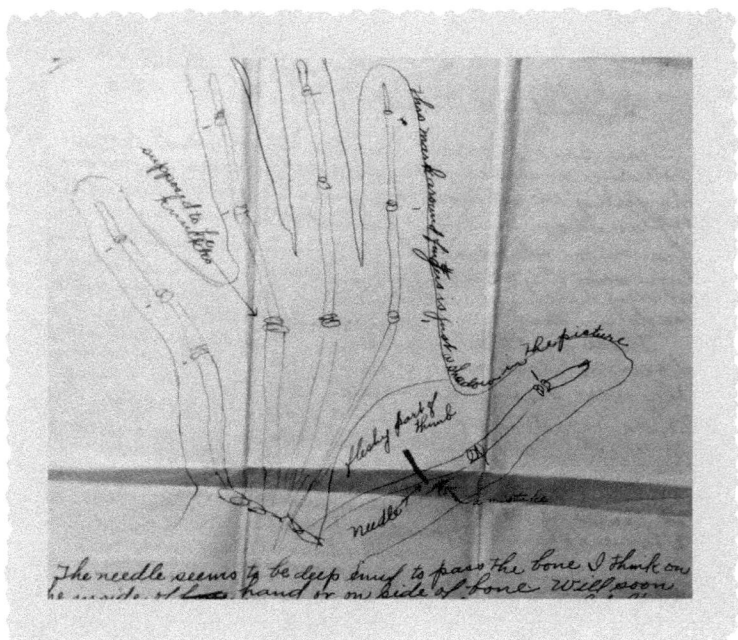

The needle seems to be deep enuf to pass the bone. I think on the inside of the hand or on side of bone. Will soon

Leora's sketch of where the needle embedded.
Sent to Delbet and Donald

Clipping: *The Sentinel*, January 10, 1935: Needle in Hand

Mrs. Clabe Wilson thinks she found something harder to locate than the proverbial "needle in the haystack" and that is—a needle in the hand! On [Saturday] morning while washing out a few things by hand she rammed the blunt end of the needle about halfway into the fleshy part of her hand, the point breaking off so that it was impossible to pull out the embedded part. The needle had been left in a dress where she had stuck it while quilting. She did not visit the doctor until afternoon and by that time the needle could not be located. It was necessary to have x-ray pictures taken to find the little steel dagger which by that time had traveled to the first joint of the thumb. An incision was made Tuesday morning and the needle removed, but Mrs. Wilson's advice to all needle users is: In the first place remove all such weapons from articles of clothing before pushing them on a washboard, and second, do not wait several hours before getting medical attention if once you get stuck with a needle.

Eggs provided the Wilsons their cheapest protein that winter, and they received some rice, canned milk, and meat from "Uncle Sam." The Navy boys sent home what money they could. "I'm telling you, we regard them as 'Life Savers'," Leora wrote. "Expect we'd have had to move in the street if we hadn't paid Hammond some to hold him off. We are lots better off than some—you boys boosting us along." They were anxious to find a place to live where Leora had enough space to raise a flock of poultry. She enjoyed raising chickens ever since childhood. She liked hearing "the singing, cackling hens."

Maybe that would happen for them during this new year.

◆

CHAPTER 29

Goffs Move to Omaha

When they first moved to Dexter, Jennings and Merl got a loan for a gravel truck. But by early 1935, job loss meant they could not keep up with payments. The Goff home had been pledged for collateral. Even after selling the truck, they failed to save the house.

After Clarence offered Jennings a job in Omaha, Jennings left on a bus right away. They planned to wait until school was out to send for the rest of the Goffs, but by mid-March they'd found a furnished house across the street from Hanscom Park large enough for all of them. It had antique furniture and chandeliers, dishes and silverware. So Grandmother, Maxine, Merrill, and Merl all moved to Omaha, leaving the furniture in the Dexter house. Grandmother reported that her new sitting room was like "entering fairyland."

The Wilson family moved into Grandmother's two-story house on the highway. They would rent there longer than any other house during those Great Depression years. Since Grandmother didn't need any of the furniture, the Wilsons used the nice four-poster beds, a heavy oak rectangular table with matching chairs and buffet, a library table, plush couch, leather prairie-style rocker—most of it from the Victorian house in Guthrie Center. This was the first house they'd lived in with indoor plumbing.

Grandmother's house along
White Pole Road, Dexter

But having her mother and brothers move left a large hole in Leora's network of support. She had almost always lived near her extended family. Two years earlier, she'd adapted to two sons leaving. Now she would have to adjust to this new emptiness.

The WPA was authorized that spring. The Works Progress Administration, part of FDR's New Deal, was designed to hire millions of unemployed (mostly unskilled men, such as Clabe Wilson) to work on public projects, including the construction of public buildings and roads.

Lone men trekked from town to town, hitchhiking when they could, looking for jobs. Grandmother's house looked promising. Once a hobo, looking especially down and out, knocked at the back door, offering to cut wood or anything in exchange for food. Leora gave him a sandwich, which he ate on the back steps. After that, men on foot seemed to stop often. Did that first man leave a message for others that that they could find food there, or was it a matter of the house being right along the highway?

This house had electricity, which meant they could enjoy listening to the radio again. With trapping money, they bought a one-piece wooden radio which sat on one end of the buffet just around the corner from the kitchen. One dollar paid for a certain amount of electricity, so they made a family rule that no one could listen to the radio alone.

The boys carved airplanes out of wood for "school exhibit" night. Danny's had pontoons instead of wheels. They'd run with their planes down the north road, propellers whirring.

Easter Sunday, Leora made rhubarb custard pies from a small mess of rhubarb that emerged every spring in Grandmother's garden. It was about time to listen to Father Coughlin. "Dad has just turned on the radio. He wouldn't miss him. Two others besides Coughlin talked, and say, they told just how history is repeating like in Christ's time. About concentrated wealth in the hands of a few, and how the money changers must be driven from the temple before prosperity and happiness come."

Back: Dale, Leora, Darlene. Middle: Clabe, Doris. Front, Junior
(holding a plane he built for "school exhibit"), Danny
Dexter, April 14, 1935

Neighbor Mary Wilt paid Dale and Danny each a quarter to pick dandelions. She and her brother Pete Jensen lived just west of Pete's pasture. The Wilson brothers weren't helping Mrs. Wilt weed her lawn. Prohibition had ended two years earlier, and she planned to use those blossoms to make dandelion wine.

The boys spent their quarters on baseball caps from the Sears catalog. Nine-year-old Junior wrote to his big brothers, "We sent out an order and I am getting a baseball cap and a pair of shoes, and I bet I'll look like a dressed up millionaire." Shoes for Dale and Danny were part of the order. Danny wrote that now they'd be able to go to Sunday School, wearing Delbert and Donald's old knickers, the ones they'd worn to eighth-grade graduation.

Leora called Junior a "corker." She mailed a photo of Dale and Darlene, saying that Dale did not want her to send it, "as he is a little shorter, you see. I said you boys ought to know about it."

Dale and Darlene. Dale is a little shorter.
"I said you boys ought to know about it."

CHAPTER 30

◆

Gossip

Donald sent $5 for Mother's Day, along with a card picturing the USS *Chicago*. "Get yourself a new hat or something, Mom." That amount could buy her "a whole outfit," she said.

When Dale learned his brothers would soon see the Hawaiian Islands, he wrote that he could hardly wait to get through school so he could join the Navy. Junior wrote, "By golly, I'm sure gonna join."

The latest allotment checks paid for rent, the light bill, and bought clothes for the kids. Clabe wrote, "You boys sure have helped us a lot." He said he finally felt better than he had in six months.

The Navy confiscated sailors' cameras when they reached the Territory of Hawaii so no military secrets would be revealed. From there the ship headed to the North Pacific drill grounds with the "greatest fleet ever assembled." Censorship controlled news about their month of maneuvers. Afterwards, they stopped at Midway Island, where the building of an American air base was underway. Delbert, his camera having been returned, sent home a photo of himself holding an albatross by its outstretched wings.

Delbert with an albatross
Midway Island 1935

Mrs. Wilt gave Leora a hen and a dozen chicks. Feeding them became part of her daily chores, including checking the tomatoes and cabbage for worm damage, along with weeding and everyday chores. Clabe got hired for part-time roadwork in the southeast part of town. At home he reset plants cut off overnight by worms, wedging slugshot around plants to try to ward off worms. They did their damage anyway.

Jennings bought a Studebaker, which he drove to Dexter to take some of the Wilsons to the Goff reunion at Springbrook State Park north of Guthrie Center. Clarence and the rest of the Omaha folks met them at the park. Boys who had jobs with the Civilian Conservation Corps, which was funded by the government, lived in barracks there and worked on buildings, trails, and bridges.

"The fear of the tongue," Willa Cather wrote, "that terror of little towns. . . . "

Clabe Wilson knew firsthand, and still smarted from it. He had tucked a June 16, 1935, clipping into a small cloth-covered New Testament, "Why Is Gossip Harmful?" At the bottom he wrote in pencil "Look it up." The Scripture noted was James 3:1-6, about the destruction the tongue can wage.

Prince Albert was Clabe's choice for pipe tobacco.
This is his pipe and the small New Testament with the clipping
still between the pages, "Why Is Gossip Harmful?"

There are several paragraphs, but Clabe had underlined part of this one: "A gossip is a public menace, and richly deserves to be muzzled; for a biting, dishonest human tongue can do more harm than the snapping jaws of a dog! A gossip can ruin your reputation, start a run on a bank, break up a church, make neighbors hate one another, shatter the happiness of a town. And no man is immune to the serpentlike flashing of a gossip's tongue."

Keeping a clipping like that says a lot about a man.

Neighbors and teachers in this small town were appreciative and supportive of the family, but a few negative comments about the Wilsons being on the dole wormed their way back. Were the comments about Clabe and the railroad incident, the family being on welfare, or both?

CHAPTER 31

◆

Clabe Becomes a Hobo

What does a man do when temperatures have reached 100 degrees, the garden has dried up, he has five kids at home, and is cut off from a government job because his two oldest sons are in the Navy?

The local canning factory might or might not have jobs. Mr. Neal, who hired the workers, promised one to Clabe if the crops were good, one for Doris as well. She hoped to earn enough money for senior pictures and a class ring.

Clabe desperately wanted work, so he started out on foot, trekking several miles into Dallas County, asking for any kind of fieldwork.

Fred Peitzman told the drifter, "Well, you are a stranger but I'll try you."

Those folks did not know what a depression was, Clabe said. They paid him $2 per day plus board. Around Dexter farmers paid $1.50 and one or two meals, but they did not want anybody staying with them. Not only that, Fred and Nellie Peitzman had running water and modern conveniences. Clabe enjoyed a refreshing bath every night.

At the end of the week the man asked if Clabe could return. Peitzman's son Dale drove Clabe to Adel, where he started walking to Dexter. Someone recognized him and gave him a ride home.

Junior had come down when the mumps before Clabe left, so he fretted over whether any more kids had become sick. Junior found he could still "warble whistle" despite having the mumps.

With earnings from the week before, Clabe took the 5:45 a.m. bus to Waukee, twenty-three miles away, then hoped to catch a ride to get closer to the Peitzman farm.

He stayed with them over the next weekend. He'd never been away from home so long. Leora worried about how he'd wash his overalls and other clothes, but he managed.

"Sure fine people and satisfied with Dad, as they wanted somebody they could trust," Leora wrote their sons. "He is standing it fine. I'm so glad and sure cheers him to feel like working and to have it to do."

Clabe pitched bundles in the field during threshing. Altogether, he must have worked for Peitzmans about a month.

With help from the three younger boys, Leora dug up sixteen or seventeen baskets of potatoes—"pretty good for the size of the patch." Clabe usually wielded the potato fork to dislodge them from the soil, but Dale could take over that job. For a fall crop, they sowed turnips where the potatoes had been.

Temperatures in Iowa soared to 100 degrees. Clarence attended a convention in Des Moines, connected with his heating business, so Maxine rode to Dexter with him. Grandmother wanted some of the Wilson kids to return to Omaha with them. Dale and Danny didn't have any good clothes but needed them for school anyway. Leora sent them up to Dewey Chiles' store to purchase Security brand overalls and shirts.

Dale and Danny visited Omaha. When they came home, Darlene and Junior took their turn and got to enjoy a circus.

"Merrill and Junior just naturally saw the city on foot," Grandmother wrote. "They even washed their hands in the Missouri River."

Clarence brought Darlene and Junior home in time for school to start. Although it was such a hot summer, his company sold furnaces faster than they could install them.

CHAPTER 32

Spats

When the next-door neighbor's Boston terrier had a single puppy, he brought it over to show the Wilsons. Doris and Dale were home and fell in love with it right away.

"It's not a purebred so we're going to sell it," Joe said. "You wouldn't want to buy it, would you?"

"How much?"

"Two dollars."

"Two dollars! Let's ask Mom."

"Well, he sure is a cute pup," she said, "but you'll have to ask your dad."

Clabe said no. It would cost too much to feed it.

Doris began to cry. So did Dale.

"Okay, okay. I can't stand for big kids to cry." Clabe suggested a deal. "If you can get the dog for a dollar, you can have it."

The neighbor accepted the dollar, and the Wilsons had a new family pet. They made a bed for him on the back porch, where he always greeted his family. Danny, in junior high that fall, arrived home from school first. The pup was so glad to see him that he leaped right into his arms.

One day, Mrs. Wilt visited with Leora when Danny reached home. They watched him hug and kiss the dog. Mrs. Wilt glanced at Leora. "Isn't that sweet?"

Darlene wrote her brothers all about school, and about the cutest puppy "a foot long and as round as a barrel. We can't get a name to suit him. If you have any suggestions, let's have them. He's kind of a light brindle with a white spot on his head, two front white paws, and the black paws just have the tips of white."

Delbert came up with the name "Spats." He and Donald had played in their uncles' uniforms from the world war, which included spats that covered a soldier's insteps and ankles.

According to ten-year-old Junior, "Spats is the best dog in the country–he's the smartest dog, too."

Top to bottom: Dale, Danny, Junior, Spats
Dexter, 1935

CHAPTER 33

◆

The Canning Factory

The Dexter Canning Factory was ready for sweetcorn in August of 1935. Now, if only it would rain and fill out the ears of corn. Besides hiring workers for the factory, O. S. Neal contracted with area farmers to grow a certain amount of corn, and periodically checked the fields. He told Leora that unless it rained that week, there would be no jobs.

Despite the 100 plus degree heat, it rained twice in one week, so the factory started up toward the end of the month.

Mr. Neal hired Clabe as a foreman, and also hired Doris. Mr. Neal's granddaughter Betty Neal, a classmate of Doris's, worked at the factory too.

In their senior pictures, Betty and Doris looked like they came from well-to-do families. Both girls missed the first two weeks of their senior year to earn enough money at the canning factory to pay for clothes, books, class rings (which cost $6.50), and senior pictures.

When a whistle blew, Clabe headed to the factory, east of town along the railroad tracks, to set things up. He weighed sugar, salt, and cornstarch, mixed them in large cookers, ready for the corn. Clabe also kept sieves clean and machinery going in the noisy, sloppy place.

Betty Neal and Doris Wilson
Dexter High School seniors 1935-1936

The other workers had an hour more until they needed to be at work, so the whistle signaled the sleeping Doris that it was time to get up.

She soon had blisters on her hands from shucking corn. Her feet and legs got so wet and it got cool at night, so Leora rigged up a laprobe for her. She wrapped her feet and legs in the oilcloth bag, which was lined with a gunny sack, then sat on the top part of it. Soon others had made similar contraptions, which they hung in the warm engine room overnight to dry.

Doris dreaded when farmers pulled up with their horses and a load of corn at sundown. Late or not, corn must be processed immediately. Otherwise the corn will spoil by heating up and causing the cans to bulge and explode after canning. Other workers cut the kernels from the corncobs. They all stayed at the job until the work was finished.

Younger siblings took turns taking dinner to Doris and her father, and a late supper for their dad when he worked into the night to get ready for the next day.

All of them toiled long hours–from 8:00 in the morning until midnight or after. Then Clabe and others stayed to wash the canning machinery and floors, scalding them with a hose, sometimes taking up to four hours longer than the shuckers.

Doris's first pay envelope for a week's work held $6.55, or 20 cents an hour. That paid for her class ring. In her second pay envelope, she had earned $12.50.

Farmer's Canning Factory, Dexter, Iowa

The canning factory job certainly helped the Wilsons pay the bills, and it provided a couple of senior girls an encouraging start to their final year in school.

CHAPTER 34

◆

New Deal Jobs

Mrs. Wilt brought Leora a big pan of apples and wanted to know, would Leora's boys go to the grain elevator and get her some wheat? And be sure to tell Delbert and Donald hello from her. She had all the apples she wanted, and the Wilsons could have the rest. Dale and Danny picked apples for their mother to preserve for winter. She also canned grapes.

The National Youth Administration was another government agency providing part-time work for needy students. Darlene worked for one of the teachers through the NYA, and the janitor assigned jobs for Dale to do.

Dale tried out for football, learning the fundamentals. He excitedly traveled to Greenfield with the team. The coach gave him a book about playing quarterback and asked him to call signals for the second team practice. Dale wasn't one to brag, but his proud mom noticed his contentment.

Junior often jogged uptown to the post office before school, just in case a letter had arrived from one of the brothers. When they received one, all five siblings listened as their mother read it before they headed out for the day.

When Clabe and sons went hunting that fall, Danny was old enough to carry a gun. He shot two squirrels with the Winchester. Clabe had demonstrated how to skin them and prepare the meat. Leora would cook anything they brought in already cleaned. Clabe readied a bunch of traps for open season, which started November 10. They'd already noted the tracks around of 'coon, skunk, and fox. Big flocks of geese headed south, a harbinger of the changing seasons.

"All I know is it sure is dead in this part of the country," a dejected Clabe wrote his sons. "Hundreds of men everywhere looking for jobs and none to be had yet. The PWA thinks there will be some work by Dec. 1 for some." The Public Works Administration was created to provide construction jobs for bridges, dams, large hospitals, etc. Clabe had registered for a job but was uncertain about getting one.

"We have made up our minds," he said, "that we are going to get out of this damn hole by spring anyway. If we can't get on a farm this spring, we are thinking of going west somewhere. I think we would be just as well off as we are here. . . . We have not got a thing to stay here for."

He'd even written the Secretary of the Interior for information on Alaska.

"Well, boys," he went on, "don't you worry about us or anything. We all will be all right as long as we are all healthy."

Dale, Danny, and Junior spent a couple of days making a clubhouse out of an old chicken house, "sounded like someone was building a new barn," according to their dad. He kidded them, saying it'd be a good place to skin the skunks.

Leora and Clabe sent an order to Sears for overshoes and socks as a surprise for the boys. Doris's new basketball shoes arrived too large for her, but she wore them anyway. Mr. Clampitt noticed that other players did not have money for decent shoes, so he bought black shoes for the whole team.

During cold weather, Leora kept a mitten box behind the kitchen stove. In the evening, Spats grabbed a mitten and nudged it against someone's knee to get them to play with him. Once Mr. Neal delivered milk to the Wilsons. Spats noticed a glove dangling from his hand, grabbed it, and off he ran to his bed on the porch. Mr. Neal knocked on the door and reported what had happened, so he could get his glove back.

Father Coughlin didn't want to oppose the president's New Deal, he insisted on his radio program. Just perfect it. He organized groups "To Keep America for America." No politics, he stressed, just justice.

CHAPTER 34—NEW DEAL JOBS

Clabe and Leora listened faithfully to this sermonizer from Royal Oak, Michigan.

Despite having so little, they probably sent a small donation to the radio priest. Why else would there be a small crucifix and a Holy Ghost charm, souvenirs of the Shrine of the Little Flower, Royal Oak among their keepsakes decades later?

Radio Priest Father Charles Coughlin

Souvenirs from Royal Oak, Michigan

Shrine of the Little Flower

Father Coughlin's ideas made great sense to families
trying to survive desperate times.

CHAPTER 35

'Possum for Birthday Dinner

Leora served roast opossum and sweet potatoes for dinner on her forty-fifth birthday. She wrote Del and Don, "We had roast coon 2 years ago today, remember?"

Dale added his own letter, "Today we had possum and sweet taters. Boy it was sure good."

Darlene wrote as well, "The sun is shining beautifully this morning. Dad and the boys are out trapping this morning, so Mom and us girls clean house and get dinner for the hungry hunters when they come. They came in with two opossum yesterday, and today we're going to have opossum and sweet taters. Yum! Yum!"

She chatted about her twin Dale playing football, older sister Doris playing basketball, younger brother Danny old enough to hunt with his dad. "Well, I'll write more after having a piece of the good opossum with the fumes just a-oozin' out, and some gravy and sweet potatoes."

Businessmen put on a football banquet at the Presbyterian church basement. Dale did not want to go because he couldn't "eat natural," but four days later, he wrote that he wished there were a banquet every night. He enjoyed eating a generous meal and listening to the senior boys' speeches. Mr. Clampitt shared his thoughts and so did a former football player from the college at Ames.

Junior dashed outside with the football nearly every morning before school. He'd kick it, then he and Spats would sprint after it.

The sole of Junior's shoe came loose, so his dad repaired it. "Quite a bunch of boys play almost every evening in Campbell's pasture or Pete's," Leora wrote. "A pretty busy football when there is not school."

Doris was too nervous to eat before basketball games. When the music for the radio show "Jack Armstrong, the All-American Boy" began, she headed for the community building for a home game.

In an early December girls' contest, Doris scored 25 out of Dexter's 29 total points. Dale, Danny, and Junior's legs dangled from the stage where they and their friends cheered on Doris. They also served as score-changers by replacing cardboard numbers with the current score.

Del and Don wrote home often. "We just couldn't stand it very good if you didn't. That's the brightest 'spot' to us—you boys' good letters."

Men with sons in the Navy or CCC lost relief jobs first, but Clabe kept busy trapping. He'd start out early by moonlight to check his traps, but he often left disappointed. Only six skunks and five opossums so far that fall. He shipped eight skunk and five opossum pelts to Sears, saying that at least it's a good healthy job.

Clarence Goff's heating business had doubled, and he expected the same for 1936. He sent his sister's family $10 for Christmas. Wayne Goff shipped a box of very welcome fruit from California, as Iowa in December is colorless, the homeliest month of the year.

Leora mailed some homemade divinity fudge to the Navy boys, just like last Christmas. They'd gathered some of the nuts in the candy from "down on Jim Creek, south of the big spring where you boys got water when you were hunting squirrels," Clabe wrote.

Delbert and Donald spent Christmas with Willis and Ann and their two daughters, Connie and Shirley, who'd asked for a Shirley Temple doll for Christmas.

Christmas Day 1935: Dan, Junior with Spats, Dale, Doris, Darlene.
Doris altered hand-me-downs so no one would
recognize who used to wear it.

CHAPTER 36

◆

Blizzards

Clabe turned forty-eight in January. Being an introvert, he did not attend the kids' ball games or many school events. He preferred spending time at home with his family, helping Leora clean and fill the kerosene lamps, keeping the wood box full, and mending someone's shoes.

Mid-January, he obtained a government job, one of the 150 WPA men working on a Dallas County crew in Redfield.

The year 1936 is still known for its temperature extremes. The week Clabe started the job, it snowed nearly a foot, and the temperature plummeted to 28 degrees below zero. That began the most frigid three weeks in Des Moines's history.

After two weeks of arctic weather, more snow swept through the area, causing a coal shortage. Clabe and Dale cut down an apple tree and hauled it home on a sled to tide the family over until they could find coal. The school closed for several days, and what coal they had was handed out to families who needed it.

The *Dallas County News*, Feb. 12, 1936: "Second Blizzard Rages. Mercury drops 30 degrees in a few hours. Train unable to get through. The WPA men cleared the road to the gravel pit near Redfield, only to have it drift shut again." *The Perry Daily Chief* reported bitter subzero weather, with the railroads trying desperately to restore service. Buses also stalled.

Clabe helped clear the road to the cemetery for a funeral. The thermometer read minus 20 degrees on Valentine's Day. Junior prepared to take a Valentine for each boy in his room at school. Leora joked, "My, haven't you any girlfriends?"

"Heck, no!" He brought home a big orange from his teacher and about ten Valentines.

Danny said his grade doesn't do such little things anymore. But his teacher gave a candy bar to each student, chocolate and black walnut, made in Drew's Candy Kitchen right there in Dexter.

Doris, Darlene, and Dale all played basketball that winter. Though a freshman, Dale suited up for games. Doris finished the season the Dexter girls' highest scorer, and she started coaching the 7th and 8th-grade girls' team. A scout from American Institute of Business in Des Moines, which had their own basketball team, told Dexter's coach that Doris was the best high school forward he'd seen, and that she could study at AIB on a basketball scholarship.

"We received a dandy good letter from Donald yesterday," Leora wrote. "Sounded like you boys were enjoying your work and learning more every day. . . . Sounds so good to hear you boys talk of more education. When one gets enough education to realize he wants to learn more that's a good sign he or she is progressing."

Dale stood four or five inches taller than his mother that spring. Soon she'd be shorter than the younger two.

By the first of March, Clabe had been working for the WPA six weeks, earning $55. It cost him $5 for rides to Redfield. "If it had not been for you boys," he wrote, "we might have frozen. It sure did take the coal. It was the worst winter for Iowa in 117 years. Some of the roads are still blocked. It is thawing now and there sure is going to be a mess and high waters."

He went on, "Nothing here for poor people. There are more people on relief in Dexter this winter than ever before. One boy speaks to me now since his folks went on relief."

Danny wrote that they'd gotten a letter from Cousin Merrill. His dad Jennings and Merl had purchased a 1936 Chevrolet truck, and Uncle Clarence had bought a new 1936 Pontiac.

Uncle Wayne also had a new car. Since the USS *Chicago* was based in southern California, Leora wished Wayne would bring his nephews back to Iowa in his new car. "My, wouldn't we have a visit!"

Hundreds of new cars drove west past the Wilson home, "one industry which is surely booming." Not everyone struggled during these Depression years.

143

CHAPTER 37

◆

Basketball Tourney

When the Dexter girls' team played at Adel, the coach bought them all Coney Island hotdog sandwiches from Mac's Cafe. Doris had never tasted one before.

Doris dislocated her ankle in a game. At a break she asked a teammate to hang onto her calf and another to yank her foot as hard as she could. "Do it again, harder!" The second time her ankle popped back into place, and she played the rest of the game with no pain.

During a tournament, Dexter and the other team stayed within one point of each other toward the end of the game. The gym was a din. When the gun went off, the other team won by one point. But the scorekeeper said the timekeeper, also from Dexter, had been caught up in the game and shot the gun off late. For the first and last time, Doris cried after the game in the locker room. They all did.

The Sentinel, March 5, 1936: "Some Kind Words. Cage Chatter in the Perry Chief of Fri. & Sat. had some nice things to say about Les Bebout & Vic Zike. But the nicest of all, we think, were these words about—well, read it: Doris Wilson,

Doris was Dexter's entrant for basketball queen for the county tournament. Dexter, 1936.

Dexter cager, has averaged 14 points per game for the last two years at the Gold & White institution. She also had established quite an enviable scholastic record with a 94 average. To top it all, Doris is Dexter's entrant for the Queen's throne!"

"[Seniors] The next senior is the one who made herself famous by her basketball career. Doris Wilson was born Aug. 30, 1918, south of Guthrie Center. At the age of five she and her parents moved to Dexter where Doris began her schooling. The Dexter schools have been glad to claim her during her twelve years of attendance. When in high school Doris participated in all outside activities except declamatory. In basketball she was especially good and her place will be mighty hard to fill. Doris says her future is uncertain but it has been said she will probably get a position on either the A.I.B basketball team or the Tulsa Stenos."

Dallas County News, Mar. 11, 1936: "Redfield had a hard time in disposing of a scrappy Dexter team, as Wilson, one of the outstanding tournament stars, hooked shots from all angles. The two left-handed forwards proved to be almost too much for Redfield and until the last quarter succeeded in keeping the Dexter team in the lead."

First all-tournament team: McClaughlin (Adel), Harper (Redfield), Wilson (Dexter), Ross (Dexter), Mabbitt (Redfield), Nevitt (Stuart).

March means mud in Iowa, but it's also a hopeful month. Buds swell and redden on the maples. Graceful willow branches add a tawny flourish. It's too soon to take down the heating stove to make more room in the living area, but wave after wave of geese flock northward, calling in the dark. Buzzards and meadowlark songs return.

The Wilsons planted greens and onions. Sometimes the weather allowed Leora to hang the washing outside to dry. Leora wondered what life would bring her oldest daughter after high school. After basketball. But at least she'd have a high school diploma. She would find her way.

CHAPTER 38

Pollywogs Become Shellbacks

"Dad always asks the first thing when he gets home from work if we've got a letter from you Navy boys." It'd been three weeks since they'd last heard from them. One of the kids checked for letters at the post office three times a day.

"Whoopee! Got a great big dandy good letter from Delbert!" He and Donald had visited their aunts and uncles, and they discussed driving back to Dexter in the fall with Uncle Wayne. "It would do you all good and you just know what a lot of good it would do us! Seems like it would be too good to be true!"

Leora cautioned them to keep their good character while on leave. "Don't pay any attention to those coast girls around shore. You are young and there are good girls somewhere always who will want good clean husbands sometime. Just watch your step and don't let anybody fool you and you'll be doing fine. <u>Don't be led astray by anyone</u>."

Delbert sent home a *Strength and Health* magazine, which included information about weightlifting. His younger brothers certainly enjoyed reading it and seeing pictures of "real men," as Dale called them.

Clabe cautioned Delbert not to increase his allotment. "You have done as much as any boy could do. You boys have been as good to your Dad and Mom as any two boys that ever lived and we know it. And so do the Kids. Spend some money on yourself, go and have a time. Don't worry about the future too much. You boys are getting an education and that is something that is a lot better than money, and not so easy to get anyway. A good strong body and an education are better than anybody's money.

"There are a lot of people right around here that had a lot of money two or three years ago that have not got a dime today. I figure there will always be money in this old world and as long as a fellow is healthy, he can get some of it."

Clabe had felt more like working that spring than he had for a long time, which meant a lot to him.

Junior and Dale played marbles with several others during dinner break at school. Dale had won about seventy of them that spring. Even Superintendent Clampitt played occasionally.

Spring meant more chores for the Dexter brothers. Neighbor Addie Creswell made them a deal. If they'd keep her yard mowed, they could use her garden for the year. Leora helped them rake it, planning to plant potatoes on Good Friday.

Earl May garden seed arrived by mail. Leora had ordered 500 Bermuda onion plants and frost-proof cabbage.

The USS *Chicago* took part in simulated naval wargames with other ships east of Panama. That May was the hottest Delbert had ever experienced. They performed watch duties below deck in 125-135 degree heat. For a breather, they stood under a blower at times, but several sailors felt ill and fainted. Most sailors slept topside.

After transiting the canal, four heavy cruisers, including the *Chicago*, headed on south to Chile for a goodwill tour. As each ship reached the Equator, it halted for the centuries-old maritime tradition of initiating the "pollywogs" upon their first crossing. During the zany ceremony, each seaman paid a visit to King Neptune (in costume) to see if they'd "qualify for entrance into the domain of Neptune." To become a "shellback," they endured some hazing and performing given silly and embarrassing tasks to carry out. Their younger brothers laughed out loud while listening to their mother read that episode to everyone.

By the end of May, the sailors savored autumn weather. Trees dropped their leaves in Valparaiso, Chile, and snow crowned the Andes Mountains. Delbert and Donald wished they could speak at least a little Spanish. Junior, having studied South America in school, asked if they saw a llama.

Delbert proved a generous son and brother. He mailed hankies to Dale, Darlene, and Danny for their May birthdays, and a decorative pink pillow cover for Mother's Day.

CHAPTER 39

◆

Another Dexter
High School Diploma

While doing road work east of town, several men, including Clabe, became "terrible sick" from drinking spring water. After Clabe recovered, he shoveled gravel at the Redfield pit.

"Van Meter has the best ball team in the county," Dale reported, "and maybe in the state. Bob Feller is their pitcher and he has already been wanted by some teams. We played them and they beat us 13-0 and didn't even try." Bob Feller became a Major League Baseball pitcher. The eventual Hall-of-Famer became known as "the Heater from Van Meter."

Dale, Danny, and Junior kept busy mowing at home, and for Hills, Addie Creswell, and Mary Wilt. They'd earned $2.60. Next came weeding the garden and picking cherries for Mrs. Wilt. Leora had canned twenty quarts of cherries so far, expecting to end up with 100 quarts. They had "green beans galore," and Junior was assigned the job of whacking dust out of the rugs draped over the clothesline.

In 1936, Doris was the third Wilson sibling to complete high school, finishing third in her class of twenty-two.

The Omaha folks spent Decoration Day in Dexter. Doris rode back with them, her first time out of the state of Iowa. They returned in time to enjoy the Goff Reunion at Springbrook Park north of Guthrie Center.

151

Omaha, 1936. Merl Goff, baby Ronnie, Bernadine (Jennings' wife,
a former Dexter teacher), Grandmother (wearing a hat),
Doris Wilson, and her cousin Maxine Goff, Jennings Goff.
Merl and Jennings are Grandmother's sons.

That summer was one of the hottest on record. Doris began working for Dr. Osborn's family for $3 per week. She'd come home and shoot baskets in such hot temperatures. "Girl, you're going to kill yourself," her mother warned.

A representative of Simpson College talked to Doris about attending college there, but she had no financial help and hardly a change of clothing. Her future seemed pretty dismal at that point.

Clipping: *The Sentinel*, June 1936. "Donald Wilson Gets Fine Promotion—Donald Wilson, enlisted in the navy and assigned to the USS Chicago, has been named to enroll at Bellevue College in Washington, DC, for a six months period, where he will take a specialized course in technical electrical instruction. The special detail is a distinct promotion for Donald and his Dexter friends will be happy in his new opportunity for advancement."

It was the first time Donald would be on his own, without his big brother around. But his folks were glad he'd be learning a trade.

◆

CHAPTER 40

California Visitors

Willis Goff's cosmetics business in California prospered so that he'd remodeled part of his store. He and Ann drove back to Iowa with their daughters, Connie and Shirley, ages nine and seven. After seeing Doris's graduation picture, they pouted that she did not look as glamorous in person. "Put on your makeup," the girls urged.

The visitors also asked for washcloths. The Wilsons' washcloths had worn out long ago, and their towels had become thin.

Even so, when the Goffs returned to California, Connie changed her doll's name to Doris.

Democrats renominated President Roosevelt in June. "There is a mysterious cycle in human events," he said in his prophetic acceptance speech. "To some generations much is given. Of other generations much is expected. This generation of Americans has a rendezvous with destiny."

The drought was severe enough that the president toured part of the Midwest.

California visitors Connie, Ann, and Shirley Goff, 1936

His train rumbled through Dexter from Atlantic so he could attend the Midwestern Drought Conference in Des Moines.

Because of the severe heat and lack of rain, work at the Dexter canning factory didn't last long that summer.

Jennings brought Grandmother and Maxine to Dexter to visit at the end of August. Maxine stayed three weeks with the Wilsons.

When Delbert got leave that fall, he and Willis caught a ride as far as Omaha. Clarence brought them on to Dexter. Willis took a bus to Detroit and two days later rolled into town with his new Chrysler Royal touring sedan. He drove Leora and Delbert to Guthrie Center the next day for dinner at Parrish's Cafe. They saw Aunt Cora and family, and Willis showed off the car in his hometown.

Delbert was home during squirrel season, so they did a little hunting down by Bear Creek, taking Spats along. They shot five squirrels, which they dressed for supper. Delbert wrote Donald how he appreciated Iowa's clear cool fall weather, great for football and hunting. He prayed for a good tracking snow while visiting, since "the fox are thicker'n flies in a cow barn when you're milking by hand."

Clipping: *The Sentinel*, November 8, 1935—"Delbert Wilson, in company with his uncle, Willis Goff of Los Angeles, California, came Sunday for a several weeks' visit in the Clabe Wilson home. Delbert, who is in the Navy and stationed on the west coast on the USS Chicago, enlisted two years and one-half ago and this is his first furlough home."

Delbert was back on the ship when Donald asked to borrow money from him to come home on leave in time for Christmas.

Clipping: *The Sentinel*, December 20, 1936—

"Donald Wilson of Bellevue, D.C., came Sunday for a three week's furlough from the navy in the parental Clabe Wilson home. When his vacation is completed he will go to the west coast, where he will again join his brother Delbert on the

USS Chicago. Donald has been in the east for several months in school at Bellevue College, Washington, DC.

"What a year 1936 proved to be! Blizzards, record cold, record heat, another Wilson finished high school, visits from Omaha and California relatives, older sons seeing interesting parts of the globe, and both of them getting to come home on leave for a short time.

Now, if only something would come up the next year, to help people find real jobs and have enough to eat.

CHAPTER 41

◆

American Institute of Business

In FDR's second inaugural address, he spoke of seeing one third of the nation "ill-housed, ill-clad, ill-nourished," and called the country to action, saying that "the test of our progress is not whether we add more to the abundance of those who have much; it is whether we provide enough for those who have too little. . . . "

"I see millions of families trying to live on incomes so meager that the pall of family disaster hangs over them day by day.

"I see millions whose daily lives in city and on farm continue under conditions labeled indecent by a so-called polite society.

"I see millions denied education, recreation, and the opportunity to better their lot

and the lot of their children.

"I see millions lacking the means to buy the products of farm and factory and by their poverty denying work and productiveness to many other millions.

"I see one-third of a nation ill-housed, ill-clad, ill-nourished."

In early 1937, the Wilson family epitomized that ill-clad and ill-nourished one third of the nation.

The American Institute of Business offered Doris a basketball scholarship. At the semester, one of the players was not working out, so they wanted someone to take her place. But what about meals and a place to stay? She could work in a downtown cafeteria for her meals and rent a room with other girls. The Wilsons trusted Mr. Clampitt who encouraged her to try it.

When a neighbor learned that Doris had packed her things in a cardboard box to take to the capital city, she loaned her a suitcase. Mr. Clampitt drove her to Des Moines and enrolled her at AIB. They found a room within walking distance, Bishop's Cafeteria hired her and issued her a uniform. And Delbert started sending $10 a month to pay for rent.

Doris had to walk downtown to work and class. She fretted about finding her way on her own.

During a drill at Doris's first basketball practice, one of the girls threw a ball so hard to her that the basketball knocked the breath out of her. She knew then which girl she would replace. When it was Doris's turn to pass to her, she gave her a dose of her own medicine. She could see on the faces of the other girls that they already enjoyed having her on the team.

AIB - American Institute of Business
Tenth and Grand, Des Moines

She didn't have a phone. Warren Neal had learned her address and showed up at her apartment to see if she'd go on a date. They'd dated some in the past, but she turned him down, too embarrassed to tell him why. She'd washed both dresses, and they were drying, so she had nothing to wear.

Good for recruitment, the AIB girls' team played at area high schools, especially the players' hometowns—Winterset, Fonda, Guthrie Center, Centerville, Dexter, Bode.

When they played at Dexter, they dropped Doris off at home. Since the family had already used up their canned goods, a meager dinner awaited them—bread, water, and brown sugar. They'd begun to burn furniture for heat.

When the grocer learned that Doris was going to AIB, he sent his wife to the Wilsons' home. She asked when Leora planned to pay their grocery bill, since they seemed to have enough money "to send a girl to college"?

An exasperated Leora set her straight.

Darlene made a dress in Home Economics that spring. Remember the pump organ that Mrs. Wilt gave the Wilson family back in 1933? Dale needed wood for a Manual Training project. No one played the organ, so he used some of it to make a radio table.

Delbert, still on the crew of the *Chicago*, made a summer cruise to British Columbia and Alaska. Every time they stopped along the west coast, he'd visit with locals about the prospects for a farm for his Iowa family. They were not very encouraging. He believed a better-paying job in California awaited when his enlistment was up, so he arranged for Donald to send rent money to Doris until he found work.

Doris never got money from Donald. He never mentioned it. She dropped out of school and left a note for her landlady, promising to pay as soon as she got a job.

Darlene and Dale with their projects, Dexter, spring 1937

Donald never explained why he had not sent money, but decades later there was evidence that he may have been gambling during that time. He owed money to Uncle Willis.

CHAPTER 42

◆

Discharged from the Navy

While still in the Navy, Delbert wrote letter after letter applying for jobs. A government position paid well and represented security, so he searched for state jobs. He knew a highway patrolman in Arizona so asked about that, but applicants had to be residents there for three years first. Iowa Electric Company hired one of Delbert's shipmates, so he wrote about a job. But they'd quit hiring and had started laying off workers.

The menu of his Iowa family's Thanksgiving dinner came mostly from their garden, but Delbert enjoyed one last feast aboard the *Chicago*. The menu included "Cream of Tomato Soup, Soda Crackers, Crisp Celery, Ripe Olives, Sweet Pickles, Lettuce and Pineapple Salad, Sweet Mayonnaise, Roast Young Turkey, Oyster Dressing, Giblet Gravy, Candied Carrots, Creamed Cauliflower, Mashed Potatoes, Cranberry Sauce, Parkerhouse Rolls, Butter, Coffee, Fruit Cake, Assorted Nuts, Ice Cream, Cigars, and Cigarettes."

By December, Delbert was a civilian. He still had hope. A crewmate hired on with five other electricians in the maintenance department of General Motors, 70 cents an hour.

Cora and John Parrish ran the Guthrie Center cafe, and they drove down to ask if Doris would like to work for them. She rode back with them, earned $1 per day plus meals, a uniform, and free rent in the apartment above the cafe.

She spent her first $10 earnings on repaying the landlady in Des Moines. After receiving it in the mail, the surprised woman wrote Doris to contact her if she ever needed housing in Des Moines again.

Great Aunt Cora asked Doris to help cut up chickens to fry, but Doris did not know where to start. "Well, I can't believe that a daughter of Leora's doesn't know how to cut up a chicken!" Doris did not reveal that her family had rarely had chicken to eat.

Every morning, Doris polished silverware for 100 customers. By Christmas, she'd saved enough tip money to buy a few Christmas gifts. She packed a few things and hiked to the train station. She had not ridden the *Liza Jane* since she was a toddler, when she stayed with her grandparents in Guthrie. The *Liza Jane* took Doris to Menlo, where she waited a couple of hours for the bus to Dexter.

Dexter Loyal Navy Mothers Club, No. 37, sent a Christmas card to Donald. "Are you a member?" Donald wrote. "I hope not. It's like some quiltin' where all the hens get together and 'yap' about each other and everybody else!" It must have worked, as Leora did not join.

Upon finishing the class, Donald was assigned to the new USS *Yorktown* (CV-5), an aircraft carrier, commissioned at the end of August. Donald tried out for the Portsmouth Cubs, a Dixie Professional League, guaranteed $15 per baseball game.

By the end of the year, Delbert still had not found a job.

CHAPTER 43

◆

California Jobs Fizzle

Donald, based in Virginia, said he'd had a pretty good season playing for the Portsmouth Cubs. They wore "classy suits. The pants were all red silk, the jerseys red with white numerals, red headgear, socks red and white circles. So you can imagine how classy the team looked. Most of the players are college graduates from the schools here in the east." No mention of sending any money.

The aircraft carrier sailed to Cuba for its two-month shakedown cruise. Donald was promoted to Electrician's Mate second class. e served as telephone electrician for the "355 automatic phones on the ship and of course all the switches and batteries." Half the crew were former farmers and had never used a telephone before enlisting in the Navy. "I'm getting them pretty well trained now."

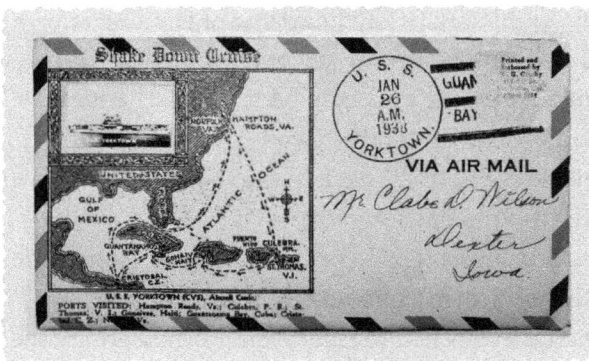

Delbert took a civil service exam, but out of 1000 who took the test, he was number 103 on the waiting list. The General Motors plant shut down, so Del's former crewmate, Bernie Bergeron, was already out of a job. At least Bernie's folks had recently relocated there from Michigan, so Delbert ate there occasionally. Delbert and Bernie visited their old ship and learned that Denison had gone home to Kansas after being discharged. However Kansas proved too cold for him so he returned to California. Delbert kept sending out applications and even took an exam hoping to qualify for State Orchardman. He wondered if he should have extended his naval enlistment.

How dispiriting for his folks to learn about their son's job struggles from afar. Surely he'd have better luck in California than in Iowa.

Three former navy pals rented a house together, checking the newspaper want-ads every day. Delbert worked a while for a brick-layer but that job soon played out. He signed up for state compensation of $10 every two weeks but had to wait two weeks for the first payment.

Finally in April, Delbert found a job repairing movie cameras for $15 per week. He carried expenses for the others since they'd assisted him for most of a month. Uncle Willis offered Del money, but he said he needed to repay the cash he'd borrowed from before.

He sure wanted to get back home, even for a short visit. "You know what would satisfy my heart more than anything else I can think of? To fill the reservoir [on the big stove, with water hauled from an outside pump] and help Mom with the washin' and chop 'n' haul wood with Dad and the Boys."

He knew he could move back home if he had to. "I reckon I could find enough to do to earn my vittles."

"The greatest successes," Leora encouraged, "sometimes are those who have some hardships in getting there."

That job fizzled. When the Denison brothers discussed returning to Kansas, they talked Del into riding along at least part way. He traveled with them to Salt Lake City, where they stayed with their sister. From there, they drove straight through. Before daylight the next morning, in western Nebraska, a tire blew out. The car rolled, ending up in a ditch, where a highway patrolman found them. After being checked out at a hospital, the Denisons sold the car and took a bus on to Kansas.

Delbert hitchhiked to Omaha, stopping long enough to call Uncle Clarence. The man who'd given him the ride drove off with Del's bag. His clothes, a camera, and the letters he'd saved from home were stolen. How disheartening.

Clarence picked up a dejected young man. Everything he had was gone, but what a great supporting network of Goffs Delbert had—in California and now in Omaha.

CHAPTER 44

◆

Bounty for Starlings

Starlings have long been considered pests, causing damage, and spreading disease. The Wilsons had seen a cloud of two thousand of the dark speckled birds, like a big swarm of bees.

Dallas County paid a ten cents per bird bounty on starlings and crows that June. Dale, just about to start his senior year, took advantage of that bounty. He'd have extra expenses, such as a senior picture and a class ring.

Dale had already bagged 36 starlings by June 3. He and his brothers had purchased a bicycle from the Freestones for $10, so he biked to Adel, seventeen miles away, with the feet as proof. He brought home $3.60.

Four days later, he again headed for Adel with evidence from 48 starlings and 3 crows. Leora watched until he returned home safely, this time with $5.10.

Halfway through June, verification from another 55 starlings biked to the county seat netted $5.50.

Three days later he brought home $4.70 cash.

Even though they'd seen another huge flock of starlings, their raucous screeching like rusty hinges, the bounty money was only good until July 1st. Dale made one more trek, bringing home $6.50 more.

Bagging 254 birds earned Dale $25.40. All that bicycle riding also got Dale in shape for fall sports.

Dale's recordkeeping of bounty money earned
June 1938

"Mom, what size shoes do you wear?" Dale opened the big *Sears, Roebuck Catalog* on the kitchen table.

"Now Dale, you're not going to spend your hard earned money on me."

"Yes, I am."

Leora nearly cried. He'd noticed the holes in the soles of her shoes, that she'd cut cardboard to fit in them.

Sturdy women's shoes cost about $3.00, or thirty starlings. And there was enough money left for a determined seventeen-year-old's senior picture and class ring.

Darlene had taken care of a neighbors' kids for several years, also saving for things she'd need as a senior.

Twelve-year-old Junior earned some money that summer, 50 cents a day, helping tear down the old Dexter hotel. The other workers called him "Swee' Pea," from Popeye cartoons because he'd wear Delbert's sailor hats to work.

You can imagine the Wilsons' excitement when they got news that Donald was coming home on leave. "Now I hope I can have all you kids here at the same time to have my dream come true," Leora wrote. "We'll get a few snapshots of the family for the first time in about 5 or 6 years. Has been over 4 years since you were all here together."

By then, Delbert worked for Uncle Clarence, hoping to earn enough from furnace work to pay for his room and board in Omaha. But most of the work went to men with families, or someone who had bought a burner he needed to pay for.

"Swee' Pea Junior, Dexter 1938

When Donald came home that July, Leora lined up her "lucky seven" and took snapshots.

Junior (13), Danny (15), Darlene (17), Dale (17),
Doris (19), Donald (21), Delbert (23)
July 4, 1938, Dexter, Iowa

169

Delbert gave up on the Omaha job. He wrote that he'd be home soon, to "get all this coal dust, ashes, and soot out of my lungs" with some long huntin' trips and working out with barbells. Donald had "ribbed the hell out of me. . . He says they make $4 to $8 a day in the Navy Yard, and I am makin' 'coolie' wages and on and on. Well, he is just about right. C.Z. [Uncle Clarence] handed me last week's pay check of $2.31."

He arrived in Dexter on the bus the day before Thanksgiving. As usual, nearly everything on the table originated in their garden, including baked onions and a salad of ground-up carrots and raisins.

The traditional Dexter-Earlham Thanksgiving football rivalry, which had been carried on at least two decades, occurred that afternoon. Dexter Athletic Field. Dexter vs. Earlham, starting whistle promptly at 2:30, 35 cents. Earlham north side. Dexter south.

Score: Dexter 12, Earlham 0.

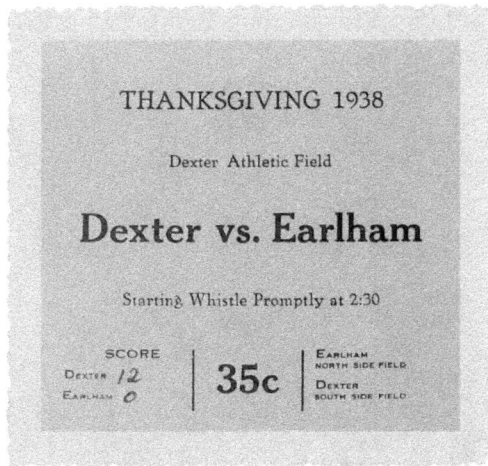

THANKSGIVING 1938

Dexter Athletic Field

Dexter vs. Earlham

Starting Whistle Promptly at 2:30

SCORE
Dexter *12*
Earlham *0*

35c

EARLHAM
NORTH SIDE FIELD

DEXTER
SOUTH SIDE FIELD

All four kids were in high school that year. Dale's football coach, Mr. Stoddard, also taught chemistry. He asked the Wilsons if they had any idea what kind of student Dale was. They knew he got good grades, but the coach said that he had to study chemistry at night to keep ahead of Dale in the classroom.

Later that year, great news was announced about a building project in town.

Redfield Review, November 28, 1938. In the Brick and Tile Center of Iowa. Dexter to Have New Community Hall—and public library. New W.P.A. allocation of federal funds to meet labor cost—to start Nov. 21. Old 2-story bank building—removed second story, rearrange ground floor—much of materials salvaged from second story. Max $6219 Federal funds for payrolls. 25 W.P.A. workmen to be used.

Work was underway on a WPA-funded job to remove the second story from a building along Dexter's Marshall Street, late 1938

Clabe began on the crew Thanksgiving week, giving the family a chance to pay some bills and buy coal for winter.

CHAPTER 45

$\Diamond$

Dallas County Champs

Dexter had a great boys' basketball squad in 1939. How heartening for the whole town of nearly 760 souls, which was still in the grips of the Great Depression. It certainly boosted the Wilson family as Dale played with the first team.

When a shoestring broke in those days, you tied it back together. Dale's broke during a game. Dexter took a time-out so he could take care of it, but it'd become so short, nothing was left to make another knot. Someone on the opposing team handed over a shoestring for him so he could finish the game.

A blizzard set in during the last game of the County Championship tournament, which was held at Perry, on the opposite side of the county. Folks at home worried the team might try to make it back in the storm, but someone sent word that they would stay overnight at the schoolhouse.

And that the Dexter boys had won the tournament!

Dallas County News, Feb. 15, 1939— "Dexter Boys Team and DeSoto Girls Are County Champs—Dexter's brilliant boys' team eked out a 21-20 victory over a strong Minburn team in the closing minutes of the championship game. It was a thrilling and exciting game all the way, and the packed house that saw

Dale Wilson, DHS
Senior 1939

it certainly got their money's worth. A crowd estimated to be over 1000 people saw the final games.

"Dexter's 'Five Iron Men' waded through all competition and then turned on the heat in the closing minutes in the last game to beat Minburn by one point. To Victor Zike and 'Homer' Harris go credit for the championship as these two hit the hoop from all angles and played a fine brand of basketball throughout the whole tourney. [Charles] Lee, [John] Shepherd and [Dale] Wilson were the other members of the team, and they, too, counted in the pinches and played great ball."

"1939 Dallas County Champions—The local boys basketball team won a hard fought game Saturday evening at the County Tournament at Perry from the Minburn quint to win the Championship. Boy, what a game. [John] Shepherd dived half way across the floor to grab the ball and save the opponents from a sure field goal. [Charles] Lee played superb ball, grabbing the ball off the bangboard many times. And [Dale] Wilson, well, if you saw that game, you know the swell game he played—a real defense man."

Funded by the WPA, local men began remodeling the two-story brick structure on the southwest corner of Marshall and Dallas streets. After removing the second story, workers transformed the first floor into a city hall, two restrooms, a community auditorium and gathering place, and a library.

The second floor had been removed, and the doorway moved from the corner to facing Marshall Street, Dexter, 1939

The supervisor's brother wanted someone to manage an eighty-acre farm near Minburn. After talking it over with Leora, Clabe took the job. Farmers readied early for spring planting. Traditional moving day was March 1. Even with the twins about to graduate, the family made arrangements to move right away. Clabe hired a truck and townspeople also helped.

Neighbors Dr. and Mrs. Robert Osborn invited Dale to stay with them to finish the year. Darlene babysat for M.M. and Zedonna Neal's boys, so they took her in.

Just ten years earlier the Wilsons had been so dispirited when all nine children suffered with whooping cough and they lost those baby twins. Then baby Marilyn died, two years later. But 1939 was certainly looking up for them. They could finally begin to save for a place of their own.

And two more Wilsons would soon be proud owners of high school diplomas.

CHAPTER 46

◆

Minburn and More Graduates

Minburn is about thirty miles northeast of Dexter, and ten miles north of Adel. The highway follows the North Raccoon River. From the Minburn depot, follow the road west of town about two miles. It curves south, then southwest, and crosses the river at the Snyder Bridge. The first road to the left is where the Wilson mailbox stood next to those of the neighbors—the Snyders, the Hoffs, the Voas'.

Take that road south about a half mile. Partway up the wooded hill to the west sat the house, with some farm buildings in the low area running to the south. The house overlooked the valley of the North Raccoon.

The day after they moved in seemed like heaven. Geese honked as they migrated in the dark. Cardinals sang boisterous spring calls all around, long before sunup. It had snowed during the night, but the day dawned bright and sunny. .

Their home-canned food had run out but, with money they'd borrowed from Mr. Neal, they bought a case of eggs from the Hoffs, at one cent each, to live on until their first paycheck. Doris helped move and said she ate three eggs at each meal, so those twelve dozen eggs did not last long. As soon as dandelion greens began to emerge, they harvested all they could.

House on the Minburn farm.
Enclosed back porch on the left, then the kitchen window, then the
dining area window. The porch on the right led to the living room

The place was rundown, with brush and weeds growing everywhere. The landlord asked them to clean up the place, promising to have the house painted and new sheds built.

The snow melted and ran under the rundown cribs. Rats scurried out. The boys shot them at night by flashlight from the back step.

As they burned brush and trash, anything that could harbor the varmints, a rat bit Spats on the nose. It made him so mad that he really tore into them from then on. Spats slept under Clabe and Leora's window.

Danny and Junior transferred to Washington Township School, west of the farm. Washington Township did not have a football team. Wanting to keep a star player, Dexter's football coach asked Danny to live with him his senior year. But Danny contentedly moved with the family.

Once they earned a paycheck, the Wilsons repaid $35 to Mr. Neal, the money they'd borrowed for groceries. They also paid the money they still owed for coal.

The Presbyterian Church hosted the Baccalaureate for Dexter's seniors. Darlene sang a solo. Four days later Mrs.Osborn drove to Minburn, nearly thirty miles from Dexter, to pick up Leora and

Doris so they could attend commencement at the Dexter Community House for the 24 graduates. Leora and Doris appreciated Mrs. Osborn's driving them so that they could attend this milestone event for two more of Leora's children.

Dale and Darlene Wilson
1939 Graduates of Dexter High School

Leora worked just as hard on the farm as she had in town, maybe harder, but enjoyed being out in the country once more. Clabe worked harder too, earned a regular paycheck, and finally seemed satisfied for the first time in over a decade.

Clabe continued to farm with horses. He rode on a two-bottom plow with an iron seat pulled by a team of five horses—two in front, three behind. The landlord provided an old truck, which Spats liked to ride in. He eventually bought a John Deere tractor, which the Wilson brothers treated like a car, washing and polishing it.

Leora did her housework with no electricity or running water at this farm, but she could afford to buy shoes and clothes. She regularly sold eggs, chickens, and butter she'd churned to a Perry grocer. The family raised a large garden, and Leora ended up canning over 1100 quarts of food that first year.

All four brothers helped their mother and farmed with their dad. The landlord continued to buy more livestock, including mules for some reason, which kept them even busier.

Donald reenlisted in the Navy, still serving on the USS *Yorktown* (CV-5). In fact, he was a plank-owner, which means served during the aircraft carrier's commissioning. He'd been playing softball with the division team, and he received a letter from Darlene. "I suppose she'll be getting married one of these days. She's the settin' hen type, you know." He said he'd sure like to be home in Iowa for squirrel hunting season.

When war broke out in Europe that fall, President Roosevelt proclaimed a "limited national emergency," and directed an increase in armed forces.

Leora wrote to both Iowa Senators, Clyde Herring and Guy Gillette, telling them they should make sure that the United States stayed out of Europe's war. The draft sent three of her brothers to France in the Great War, and she thought the nation should stay out of this one. Both senators replied with form letters.

Doris did not return to AIB. She'd noticed that secretaries, who'd gone to school there, had to watch their pennies at the cafeteria. They had to buy clothes nice enough for work, while Doris was furnished a uniform and her meals were free. She continued to waitress, first at Parrish's in Guthrie Center, a short time at the Perry's Pattee Hotel, then worked in the restaurant section of McDonald Drug.

Pohle Appliances in Dexter chose Darlene to represent them in a beauty parade at the Stuart Theater.

Clipping: *Dexter Journal*, August 4, 1939—Darlene Wilson Wins Title of Miss Dexter in Beauty Parade at Stuart—At the Beauty Parade held at Stuart Thursday of last week, Miss Darlene Wilson, former basketball star, won the title of Miss Dexter, wearing the ribbon of Pohle's Appliance store. . ."

Darlene hired out to do housework for families with a new baby or needing help, as far away as Menlo and Casey, staying with the family as well. In the spring of 1941, she married Alvin "Sam" Scar, who farmed near Earlham.

Dale found part-time work when he could. He'd never milked a cow before, but that became his job for neighbor Howard Hill. Cows must be milked twice a day. By the time Dale had finished milking each animal in the herd, one by one, it was nearly time to start again. His hands and forearms swelled nearly double. He couldn't sleep, but he refused to quit.

Because he owned a suit, Dale also worked for an undertaker, until he noticed him eating chocolates while working on a corpse.

Clabe and his sons pooled their money and bought a second-hand wine-colored Buick.

Danny, Junior, Delbert and Dale with the Buick, ready to go to the Air Olympics at the Des Moines airport, June 22, 1941

Wilson at the Minburn farm, Leora fulfilled her goal of seeing all her children earn their diplomas. Danny played basketball at Washington Township School and graduated valedictorian of the Class of 1941. Junior also played basketball, and finished his studies in 1942.

Graduates of Washington Township School
1941 - Danny Wilson, 1942 - Junior Wilson

CHAPTER 47

$\Diamond$

Leora

After a dozen Iowa autumns had come and gone, the Wilson siblings had very little in terms of memories of a house they grew up in. There had been so many—three farms and five houses, according to Doris's reckoning.

Leora's upbringing years had been similar, always moving with a large family, although she had not grown up in poverty.

Her own father had valued hard work more than an education. Of his ten children, only the two youngest completed high school. They were also the only ones who owned small businesses and thrived despite the Great Depression.

That was not lost on their eldest sister Leora, who was also blessed by the generous gifts to her family, monetarily but also in the kindred warmth shown to her young sons.

Leora's hope of a place of their own near family was only partially fulfilled. All but Donald lived at the farm. The steady income was so reassuring, and to not have to worry about growing kids getting enough to eat.

Living in plenty, the freedom of outdoors, worthwhile work, and reliable refuge gave them such hope. The landlord did have the house painted for them and added a front stoop.

Every day Leora grew closer to that goal of a place of their own. The worst of the Great Depression was behind them. Such relief!

And here they were, surrounded by the beauty of the timber each exhilarating season of Iowa's year.

Afterword: How I Learned Everything

While researching genealogy, I asked Grandma Leora to write her memoirs, and she did. I transcribed them to share with the entire family.

Before the internet, Mom and I looked through microfilm of old Dexter newspapers at the Iowa State Historical Library, searching for details about the family. Mom told stories from her growing up years and, instead of becoming bored like I did when I was younger, I took notes. Where did you live when that story happened? I sorted them house by house, slipping the notes into file folders. (I have three four-drawer filing cabinets.)

We also visited the places Leora talked about in her memoirs, at least we'd try to find them.

Old photos themselves stirred up memories, and more stories. They simmered in boxes and folders until time for them to become a narrative of the Great Depression years of the Wilson family of Dexter, Iowa.

Notes

Across the road south of where Penn Township School stood a two-story clapboard farmhouse, where I grew up in the 1950s and early 1960s.

None of the houses the Wilsons lived in still exist except for "Grandmother's house," which is across the highway south of the Dexter Park.

The big brick schoolhouse has been replaced by a one-story building.

The Methodist Church still stands.

Evelyn Corrie grew up to be Evelyn Birkby (1919-2021), a writer and broadcaster for KMA Radio and Kitchen-Klatter for decades. She also wrote several books, including the popular *Up a County Lane Cookbook*.

The truth about Samuel Wilson being an Indian Agent: One of his sons, born in 1856, learned to walk on the reservation at Ft. Omaha. An old county history said that Samuel had indeed located among Indians in Nebraska, with whom he'd spent his early life, but nothing about being an official Indian agent.

White Pole Road: Before Interstate 80 was built across Iowa, White Pole Road had plenty of traffic through town. But these days, the White Pole Road Development Corporation keeps those poles painted white between Dexter and Adair, to promote tourism for five small towns with populations of 348 in the smallest (Menlo) to 1695 in the largest (Stuart).

When Grandma Leora stayed with us at the farm and saw me park a sewing needle in the arm of a sofa. She showed me the scars in her right hand, which she could not flatten ever since 1935, caused by parking a needle where it should not have been.

The 1916 Dexter Community House, also known as "the Roundhouse," has been on the National Register of Historic Places since 1975. Built in 1916 at a cost of $10,000, elliptical in shape, the building constructed of hollow blocks, the roof is dome-shaped without a single support except at the walls. The architect was Maj. Matthew Leander King.

The Presbyterian church, which still stands, held a banquet for fathers and sons in the fall through the decades.

Great Grandmother Laura Goff's Mrs. Potts sadiron is now owned by the Dexter Museum.

The Dexter Library and Community Hall, remodeled with WPA funds in 1939, was the library I frequented as a child. I attended a junior high Valentine dance there.

This plaque is displayed inside the Dexter Public Library.

Springbrook State Park, with a spring-fed lake north of Guthrie Center, was acquired by Iowa in 1926 and most of the buildings were constructed by the Civilian Conservation Corps in the 1930s.

Bob Feller joined the major leagues even before graduating from high school, pitching 18 seasons for the Cleveland Indians. He missed prime baseball seasons by serving in WWII. Feller was elected to the National Baseball Hall of Fame in 1962.

Dutch Reagan and WHO-Radio. Ronald Reagan was a sports broadcaster before he became an actor, and later President of the United States.

Betty Neal, who worked at the canning factory with Doris, became her sister-in-law in 1943. Betty sang at the wedding. Doris married Warren Neal, who stopped by when her older brothers were home on leave, to see how they liked the navy.

Drew's Candy Kitchen is still on the west edge of Dexter. Helen Drew made her first trays of black walnut fudge in 1927, and eventually shipped all sorts of varieties worldwide, especially at Christmas time. For decades, Leora Wilson sent Drews chocolates to her West Coast relatives, and shipped some to my husband in Vietnam for Christmas 1970.

Francis Shepherd was the Guthrie Center girls' basketball coach when Dexter beat them. In 1937 the Guthrie Center girls won the Iowa State Championship. They not only got to meet Ronald "Dutch" Reagan, a sportscaster for WHO-Radio, their expenses were paid for a trip to Wichita, Kansas, to watch the AAU Women's National Championship Basketball tournament. Doris Wilson played in the tournament on the AIB team.

When Donald Wilson joined the crew of the new USS *Yorktown* (CV-5) before the ship's commissioning, that made him a "plank owner." Uncle Don served on the aircraft carrier "her whole life," as the ship was sunk during the Battle of Midway in 1942.

◆

Leora's Letters: The Story of Love and Loss For An Iowa Family During World War II tells their poignant family story during the war. All five brothers served. Only two came home.

Written with coauthor Robin Grunder, *Leora's Letters* is available in paperback, ebook, and audiobook through Amazon. Beaverdale Books (515-279-5400) will ship autographed copies of the paperback.

Leora's Letters is the story behind the Wilson brothers who are featured in the Dallas County Freedom Rock at Minburn, Iowa.

Ray "Bubba" Sorensen is the founder and artist of the 99 Iowa Freedom Rocks, one in each county. These Iowa treasures promote tourism and well as celebrating and remembering the service of hundreds of Iowans.

Questions to Ponder

1. Leora was blessed by having the support system of family, even her parents and adult siblings living nearby. At what points in the story does she have to let go of a family member? How do those losses affect her? What does that say about her character?

2. Marilynne Robinson, through a character in her book *Gilead*, says, "It is a good thing to know what it is to be poor, and a better thing if you can do it in company." Do you agree that it's a good thing to know what it is to be poor?

3. A character in Willia Cather's *My Antonia* says, "But, you see, a body never knows what traits poverty might bring out in 'em." Having lived through the challenges of 2020 (COVID-19, hurricanes, a derecho storm in the Midwest, an especially contentious election), what traits have those brought out in you?

4. In *Song of the Lark*, Willa Cather says, "The fear of the tongue, that terror of little towns. . . . " If you've lived in a small town, what are the drawbacks? What about the benefits?

5. ". . .[T]he depression that began in 1929. . . came on harder and faster, it engulfed a larger part of the population, it lasted much longer, and it did far more and far worse damage than any before it."

    In *Brother, Can You Spare a Dime*, Melton Meltzer said that no one can understand America today without knowing something about the Great Depression of the 1930s. "The deepest wounds of the depression were borne by children."

    Do you have family stories that have come down from those Great Depression years?

6. I've heard that people tend to collect or hoard the things they missed out on as children. My mother Doris could not have enough towels and sheets in the linen closet. She also collected dolls. Can you relate to this?

7. There have been times in our history where world crises create such an undertow that it affects individual lives. Besides the Great Depression and COVID-19, can you think of other events that have been turning points in your own life?

8. "The way I see it," says Billie Jo in Karen Hesse's Newbery Medal Winner Out of the Dust, (changed to one sentence from poetic lines) "hard times aren't only about money, or drought, or dust. Hard times are about losing spirit, and hope, and what happens when dreams dry up."

   Which do you think is harder: poverty of material things or poverty of spirit?

Acknowledgements

A big thank you to readers who invested time to comb through the manuscript and offer feedback, some of whom were cheerleaders for *Leora's Letters* two years ago. Even earlier, subscribers to my website were so encouraging about the embryo sketches that eventually multiplied into *Leora's Dexter Stories*.

Among the latest encouragers are avid readers, librarians, historians, military veterans, a former pastor, genealogists, Dexter Museum Board members, a coach, the administrator of the Iowans Making History Facebook page, and a former sheriff:

Marilyn Bode, Chad Brown, Jorja Dogic, Doris Feller, Louise Hartman, Pat Hochstetler, Tom Honz, Mary McCollogh, Gloria Neal, and Bryon Weesner.

Some are also authors with their own books:

» Elaine Briggs, author of *Joe Dew: A Wonderful Life*. (Elaine's father grew up at Redfield while the Wilson kids grew up in neighboring Dexter.)

» Anne Clare, author of the WWII historical novel, *Whom Shall I Fear*

» Mike Flinn, author of *May Angels Fly With You*, historical fiction set during the Great Depression, and other books

» Robert Frohlich, author of *Aimless Life, Awesome God*

» Richard L. Muniz, penname Willam R. Ablan, author of "The Lawman" series

» Dennis L. Peterson, author of *Look Unto the Hills: Stories of Growing Up in Rural East Tennessee* and other books

» Patti Stockdale, author of the WWI historical novel, *Three Little Things*

To those professionals who took the time to endorse *Leora's Dexter Stories.*

To John Busbee, delightful mentor and motivator, is a creative project developer and founder of The Culture Buzz. Trained in both theater design and arts management, he has reviewed theater for almost 20 years. With more than 150 professional and local stage credits, John coached teams for several years for IHSSA in musical theater, including multiple All-State invitations. Since 2007, John has produced an arts and culture radio program on KFMG 98.9 FM, which focuses on promoting Central Iowa's cultural scene. His work in the arts was recognized with the 2014 Iowa Governor Award for Collaboration & Partnership in the Arts.

To Guy Kidney, steadfast chauffeur

Five brothers served. Only two came home.

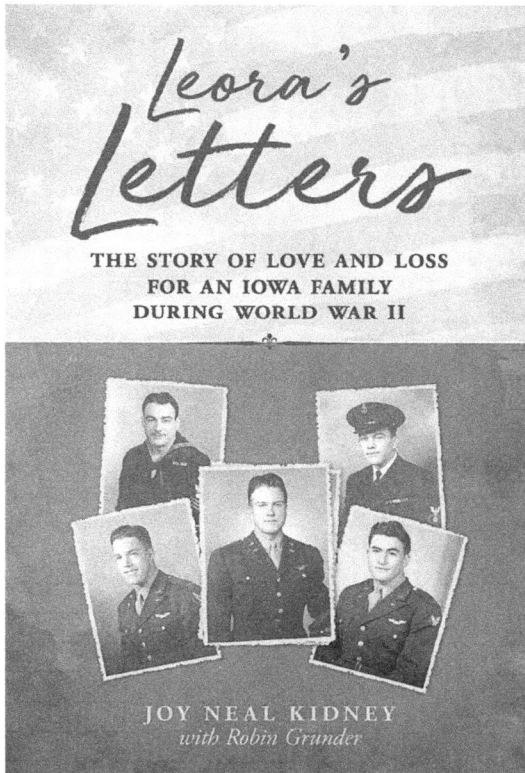

Little House on the Prairie meets *Our Town*
—John Busbee, The Culture Buzz

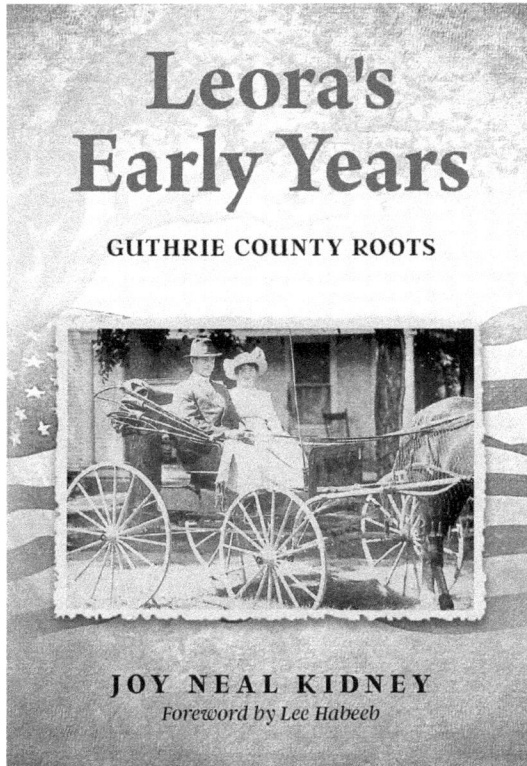

Hardbacks, paperbacks, ebooks, and audiobooks are available from Amazon.com.

Also from the Machine Shed Restaurant (autographed), Urbandale, Iowa.

Autographed and shipped paperbacks are available from Beaverdale Books, Des Moines. (515) 279-5400, beaverdalebooks@gmail.com.

Also from Off the Rails Quilting, Bondurant, Iowa. (515) 967-3550, offtherailsquilting.com.

"We must never forget these three brothers."
—Marcus Brotherton, New York Times bestselling author

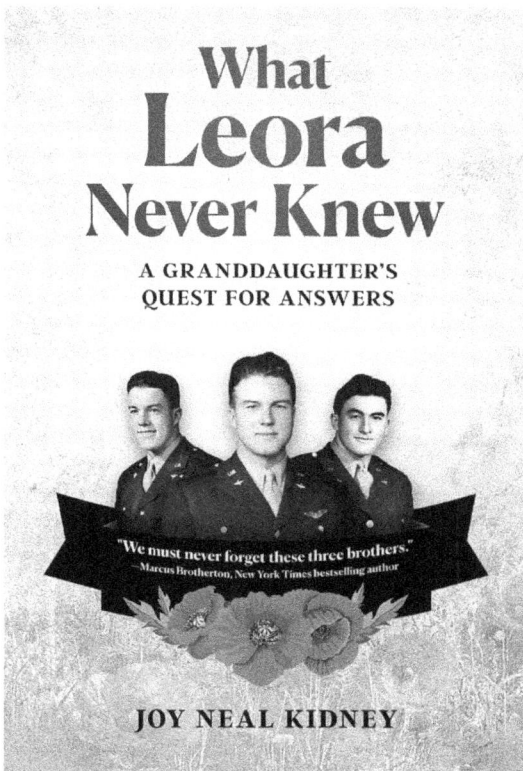

Hardbacks, paperbacks, ebooks, and audiobooks are available from Amazon.com.

Also from the Machine Shed Restaurant (autographed), Urbandale, Iowa.

Autographed and shipped paperbacks are available from Beaverdale Books, Des Moines. (515) 279-5400, beaverdalebooks@gmail.com.

Also from Off the Rails Quilting, Bondurant, Iowa. (515) 967-3550, offtherailsquilting.com.

www.ingramcontent.com/pod-product-compliance
Lightning Source LLC
Chambersburg PA
CBHW051724040426

42447CB00008B/967